6.4.76
PHOENIX
SUNS
VS.
BOSTON
CELTICS

6.4.76
PHOENIX
SUNS
VS.
BOSTON
CELTICS

The Greatest Game Ever Played

ROGER GORDON

6.4.76 PHOENIX SUNS VS. BOSTON CELTICS
THE GREATEST GAME EVER PLAYED

Author photo by Lee Spencer

iUniverse books may be ordered through booksellers or by contacting:

iUniverse
1663 Liberty Drive
Bloomington, IN 47403
www.iuniverse.com
844-349-9409

ISBN: 978-1-6632-0673-2 (sc)
ISBN: 978-1-6632-0674-9 (e)

Library of Congress Control Number: 2020914637

Print information available on the last page.

iUniverse rev. date: 08/26/2020

CONTENTS

PREFACE

What makes a great basketball game? Talented players. Great shots. Amazing passes. Slick moves. Tremendous hustle. A large lead. A fantastic comeback. An overtime period. Another overtime period. Yet another overtime period. A sellout crowd in a celebrated arena. Fans rushing the court. One of those fans attacking an referee.

A National Basketball Association game between the Phoenix Suns and Boston Celtics almost 45 years ago had all of those things and more. No, it was not a Game 7. Nor was it a Game 6. It didn't matter. This is the story of what is widely regarded as "The Greatest Game Ever Played," Game 5 of the 1976 NBA Finals. In 1996, Classic Sports Network (now ESPN Classic) polled NBA writers, and they voted the contest as the greatest single game in the then 50-year history of the league.

Played exactly one month before the nation's Bicentennial celebration, the game began just after 9 p.m. on Friday night, June 4, but due to its length, spilled over into Saturday, June 5. It was played in the historic Boston Garden before a crowd of 15,320. The Celtics won, 128–126, in triple overtime.

There were so many twists and turns during the game. In the overtime sessions, several players on both sides hit baskets that looked impossible to make. Towards the end of the second overtime, Boston's John Havlicek drove to the hoop and banked in a shot as the clock hit 0:00. Mayhem ensued. Hundreds of crazed Celtics fans rushed the court to celebrate what they thought was a victory and a 3–2 Boston lead in the series (which the Celtics went on to win in six games). It was a much different time in the 1970s, that's for sure. After much confusion, it was determined that one second be put back on the clock. One fan was so upset, he assaulted referee Richie Powers! The court was eventually cleared, and the Suns got one last shot. Gar Heard threw up a turnaround 20-foot prayer that fell through the hoop, forcing a third overtime. In that third extra period,

Sun —and ex-Celtic—Paul Westphal made some ridiculous shots that were Globetrotter-worthy.

When the game finally ended at 12:08 a.m., five players—two Suns and three Celtics—had fouled out. Boston backups Jim Ard and Glenn McDonald had been thrust into playing crucial minutes and came through with flying colors. The players were physically drained. The players, coaches, and even the fans were emotionally drained.

The Celtics, who finished 54–28 during the regular season and were heavy favorites to win their record 13th NBA title, had greats—and future Hall of Famers—such as Havlicek, Dave Cowens, Jo Jo White, and ex-Sun Charlie Scott. The Suns, in just their eighth season, won only 42 games during the regular part of the schedule. It was just their second postseason appearance ever. They were led by Heard, Westphal, and Rookie of the Year Alvan Adams.

What makes this remarkable basketball game even more special to me is the fact that it was the very first sporting event I remember watching on television, as I was nine years old at the time. There were many thrilling NBA games prior to June 4, 1976, and there have been many since, but I believe this Phoenix-Boston classic will continue to stand the test of time as "The Greatest Game Ever Played."

ACKNOWLEDGMENTS

I would like to thank everyone at iUniverse in helping me put this book together. I would like to thank Ken Samelson for his outstanding editing and proofreading. I would also like to thank the many people I interviewed, especially Bob Ryan, Tom Heinsohn, and Al McCoy.

PREGAME

Al Bianchi made sure he wore his old sport coat. "It was the one I wore when I didn't care if they threw beer on me," he said.

"They" were Boston Celtics fans. Bianchi, the Phoenix Suns' assistant coach, was preparing for Game 5 of the 1976 NBA Finals at the Boston Garden. "I knew, since the game didn't start until after nine o'clock, they'd been out to dinner drinking," he remembered.

"Everybody was hammered," recalled Phoenix radio broadcaster Al McCoy.

The series was tied, 2–2. The Celtics had won Games 1 and 2 at the Garden before the Suns took Games 3 and 4 at the Arizona Veterans Memorial Coliseum in Phoenix. The winner of Game 5 would have the inside track to the championship. "We knew we couldn't afford to lose because, if we did, even if we won Game 6 in Phoenix, we'd have to go back to Boston for Game 7. And anything can happen in a Game 7," said Celtics backup center Steve Kuberski.

This was old hat for Boston. The Celtics were aiming for their 13th NBA title, while this was just the Suns' second postseason appearance in their eight-year history. "I remember looking over at [Celtics general manager] Red [Auerbach]," recalled Phoenix general manager Jerry Colangelo, one of many players, coaches, and executives who shared their memories in a *Boston Globe* story about the 25th anniversary of that historic game published on June 3, 2001. "This was my first Finals. It was just another Finals for him, something he had experienced many, many times. I was wondering what it would feel like to be in that position."

"This wasn't Boston, with all its history," Suns shooting guard Dick Van Arsdale said about the streets of Phoenix being empty the night of the game in the same article. "This was Phoenix. This series was the biggest sporting event in the history of the city."

"This was a real shot for the Suns," said Bob Ryan, the Celtics beat writer for the *Globe*.

Ed Searcy, a reserve small forward for Boston for a small portion of the 1975–76 regular season, said that, for that Suns team to be in the NBA championship series, they were very good.

The scene was set. The Suns and Celtics were braced for battle.

"The Boston Garden was ancient, and I just loved the setting," said Alvan Adams, Phoenix's rookie starting center.

"We were ready to take them on in Boston!" declared Suns forward Curtis Perry.

Recalled Suns head coach John MacLeod in the *Globe*, "I remember taking the floor. I never heard a buzz like that."

2

THE SORRY SUNS

The Suns' road to Game 5 of the 1976 NBA Finals was not a long one, but not a happy one either. Like most expansion teams, the 1968–69 Suns had a rough go of it. Under former Chicago Bulls head coach Johnny Kerr, they won their very first game, 116–107, over the Seattle SuperSonics and actually split their first 10 games. Then reality set in. Beginning with a 111–109 loss to the Detroit Pistons in Tucson, Arizona, they lost 12 games in a row to fall to 5–17. The losing streak ended on December 4 with a resounding 126–97 victory over the San Francisco Warriors. Phoenix got right back on the losing track, though, and, after a 117–93 defeat at the hands of the Warriors on January 26, stood at 10–42. Then two victories over Milwaukee and a win over Philadelphia gave the Suns their first three-game winning streak of the season. Unfortunately, they would win only three more games the rest of the season. They wound up with an NBA-worst 16–66 record and in last place in the Western Division.

Believe it or not, there were bright spots for Phoenix, including point guard Gail Goodrich, whom the Suns selected from the Los Angeles Lakers in the 1968 NBA expansion draft. "Gail was a legitimate 20-point scorer," said Jerry Colangelo, who was Phoenix's general manager from that very first season of 1968–69 through 1993–94. "He stepped right in and, given that opportunity to start, was a prolific scorer and did a great job for us."

Averaging 21 points, 6.9 rebounds, and 4.8 assists per game was Dick Van Arsdale, "The Original Sun," whom Phoenix also chose in the expansion draft.

Other key contributors were centers Jim Fox and George Wilson, rookie power forward Gary Gregor, and veteran small forward McCoy McLemore.

"George gave the Suns some veteran help both on the floor and in the locker room," said Al McCoy. "Gary was a very heads-up, knowledgeable, smart type of player, and McCoy McLemore provided some size."

The signing of small forward Connie Hawkins, along with Van Arsdale and Goodrich, gave Phoenix a strong one-two-three punch in 1969–70. The acquisition of veteran power forward Paul Silas in a trade with Atlanta also helped. It was an up-and-down season of streaks. The Suns started 1–4 and dropped to 7–15 before winning seven of nine games to get to 14–17 after a 126–110 home win over the Cincinnati Royals on December 13. Then they lost 10 of 13 games to fall to 17–27 nine days into the new decade. They won 12 of 18 to improve to 29–33, then dropped four straight before winning 10 of 16 to finish the regular season with a 39–43 record, good enough for fourth place in the Western Division and a playoff berth to boot. The 23-win improvement was the biggest one-season turnaround in the history of the NBA at that point.

Hawkins averaged 24.6 points and 10.4 rebounds per game. "Connie was transformational. He gave us great credibility. He put us on the map," said Colangelo, who took over the coaching duties for the final 44 games of the regular season and the playoffs. "I pushed him extremely hard to do what I felt he was capable of doing."

"Connie was one of the showmen, one of the guys who did things that most players didn't do at that time," said Rick Barry, who played against Hawkins in both the NBA and the American Basketball Association. "He had a little bit of that Globetrotter stuff in him. He was a heck of a talent. He could get to the basket, could finish with excitement. He did amazing things above the rim. Most people didn't really get a chance to see him and see what he was capable of doing."

"'Hawk' had big hands. He was a good passer, too," Van Arsdale said.

"He was one of a kind," said John Wetzel, who would join the Suns the next season and have two stints with the team in the 1970s. "He was a guy who became Phoenix's identity. He was Dr. J. before Dr. J."

"Connie was one of the greatest ever to lace 'em up," McCoy added.

Also in 1969–70, Van Arsdale averaged 21.3 points per game, Goodrich hung up 20 points per contest, and Silas averaged 12.8 points and 11.7 rebounds per game.

"Dick provided veteran strength for the Suns in the early years," said McCoy.

Added Colangelo, "He was a shooter, a prolific jump shooter. He certainly helped us early on when we were establishing ourselves as a franchise."

Other key contributors were Fox, shooting guard Dick Snyder, rookie center Neal Walk, small forward Jerry Chambers, and shooting guard Art Harris.

"Neal could score, had a nice touch for a big man, had a little running hook, and could shoot the 15- or 16-foot jump shot," said Wetzel. "He was a good player."

"Neal was an outstanding center," McCoy said.

"Art and I used to go into the game together and kind of disrupt a little bit defensively," said Wetzel. "We were both aggressive defenders. Art was a good player, a high-energy guy. He could handle the ball and get to the rim."

The Suns nearly pulled off a shocker in the first round of the playoffs against Wilt Chamberlain, Jerry West, Elgin Baylor, and the Los Angeles Lakers. They took a 3–1 series lead before Fox hurt his ankle and missed their 138–121 Game 5 loss. He returned for Games 6 and 7 but was not 100 percent healthy. The Suns lost both games and were ousted from the playoffs.

"I think the jump from year one to year two in accomplishing what we did was extraordinary," said Colangelo. "And then the selection of Cotton Fitzsimmons as our new head coach coming from Kansas State … he was the right fit for when you look at the talent that we had. Neal was a very good low-post, even high-post, center. And Cotton used the triple-post offense, which was inaugurated by Tex Winter, the coach who preceded him at Kansas State. And with Paul, who was a perfect power forward, and 'Hawk,' who was the other scoring forward, we were in good shape."

Gone in 1970–71 was Goodrich, who was traded to Los Angeles for 7-foot, 230-pound veteran center Mel Counts. Two additions were guards Clem Haskins and Wetzel. The 6-foot-3, 195-pound Haskins arrived by way of a trade with Chicago. Wetzel had been property of the Suns ever since they selected him from Los Angeles in the 1968 expansion draft.

"Clem was a great jump shooter," said Colangelo. "He was a very important piece to what we had at that time. I was very high on him and his abilities."

"He was a very good guard with good size, the type of player as a coach you'd be happy to have on your team," Barry said.

"Clem had a real smooth stroke," added Wetzel.

The 1970–71 Suns began the season by losing six of their first nine games, but soon turned it around. A 110–102 home win over the Buffalo Braves on November 2 fueled a four-game winning streak and seven victories in eight games. Defeats to New York, Detroit, and Baltimore evened Phoenix's record at 10–10. Then the Suns won 10 of their next 15 games to improve to 20–15 a week before the Christmas holiday. They would never look back. They would stay above the .500 mark the rest of the season. In fact, they stood at 45–28 after a 114–108 road win over the Pistons on March 9. Under the new format that now had an Eastern Conference and a Western Conference, the Suns wound up 48–34 and in third place in the West's Midwest Division, three games behind the second-place Bulls. However, because the new format awarded postseason berths to only the top two teams in each of the four divisions, they had to sit home while 41–41 San Francisco, which finished second in the Pacific Division, qualified for the playoffs.

"It was frustrating, that's for sure," said Colangelo.

"That triple-post offense was quite effective. I thought we were really good," Wetzel said. "And we were good because there was an attitude of unselfishness, an attitude of playing together, an attitude of playing hard all the time."

Leading the way for Phoenix were Van Arsdale, who averaged 21.9 points per game, and Hawkins, who netted 20.9 points and 9.1 rebounds per game. Haskins averaged 17.8 points per contest.

In 1971–72, Phoenix improved by a game to 49–33 – highlighted by an eight-game winning streak early in the season – but again finished in third place in the Midwest Division, eight games in back of second-place Chicago, thus leaving them out of the postseason party once again. Despite the disappointment, a huge addition to the team—albeit on March 14, near the end of the season— was guard Charlie Scott. Scott was obtained in a trade with Boston for Silas and cash. Rookie point guard Mo Layton was also a key contributor.

"Mo was a little bit sneaky," said Wetzel. "You looked at him and you didn't think he was such a good athlete, but he had a knack for getting to places on the floor that he wanted to. He had deceptive quickness. I think he surprised a lot of people who were guarding him. He was a nice player."

Under new head coach Butch van Breda Kolff and Colangelo, who replaced the former seven games into the schedule, Phoenix slipped to 38–44 in 1972–73 and another third-place finish, nine games behind second-place Golden State, but this time in the Pacific Division, the team's new home. Scott, though, averaged 25.3 points and 6.1 assists per game. Walk had a magnificent season, averaging 20.2 points and 12.4 rebounds per contest.

There was a new head coach in town in 1973–74. John MacLeod was his name, reviving the Suns his game. The 36-year-old came from the University of Oklahoma, where he led the Sooners to three near-20-win seasons in six years as head coach. "In selecting John as the head coach, I just felt that he had great potential, he was so focused on the game, and he was a student of the game. And so I thought he was the right guy," said Colangelo.

Two additions to the Suns in 1973–74 were veteran small forward Keith Erickson and rookie forward Mike Bantom. Erickson arrived 10 games into the season by way of a trade with the Lakers involving Connie Hawkins. Bantom was Phoenix's first-round draft pick out of St. Joseph's.

"Keith was a multiple-skilled player who could play two or three positions," said Colangelo. "He'd developed an outside shot, which he didn't have when he first came into the league. When I was in Chicago for the startup of the Bulls in '66, we took him in the expansion draft, so I had a pretty good feel for him. He was excellent defensively, a real team player. He was very, very valuable to our club."

"Keith was smart, knew how to play the game," Barry said. "He could play some defense and was a good all-around player."

"Mike had good size, good wingspan, and could run pretty well for a big guy," said Wetzel.

MacLeod's first Suns team got off to a terrible start, dropping 18 of its first 25 games, which included a 10-game losing streak. The Suns had a decent middle third of the season. They were 22–32 following a 119–112 victory over Los Angeles on February 2. However, five- and seven-game losing streaks contributed to a 30–52 final record and fourth place in the Pacific Division. Scott averaged 25.4 points per game.

New to Phoenix in 1974–75 was Curtis Perry, center Dennis Awtrey, and shooting guard Nate Hawthorne. All three arrived by way of a trade that sent Walk to the expansion New Orleans Jazz. Also new to the team was small forward Fred Saunders, a second-round draft pick out of Syracuse University.

The 1974–75 Suns were actually enjoying a pretty good season, relatively speaking, when a 10-game losing streak dropped them from 29–35 on March 6 to 29–45 on March 22. They ended up 32–50 and in fourth place in the Pacific, just two games better than the previous season. Perry averaged a double-double—13.4 points and 11.9 rebounds per game.

"Curtis was a good rebounder and could shoot the ball when he needed to. He just played a good all-around game," said Awtrey. "He was an asset to the team. Psychologically, he was a good guy to have with you."

"He could also play defense," Barry said. "Dennis wasn't very athletic but could shoot the ball, do some rebounding, and play some defense."

"Dennis was tough and had a good knowledge of the game," added Saunders. "Nate could jump, and he could shoot the ball if he had enough time."

"Nate was a tremendous leaper and was a contributor," Perry said.

"That '74–'75 season was frustrating for everybody," said Awtrey. "We weren't playing well as a team and losing makes it seem like the season is 200 games instead of 82. Losing grinds you up."

Said Colangelo, "John's first two seasons as head coach were a learning experience for him in terms of coaching at the professional level and getting acquainted with the personnel not only on our team but players throughout the league. And that was the price of admission."

3

DYNASTY

The Celtics' path to Game 5 of the 1976 NBA Finals was a long one and a happy one. However, their first four seasons from 1946–47 to 1949–50, the first three of which were in what was then called the Basketball Association of America, produced no winning records and just one postseason berth under head coaches John Russell and Alvin Julian. Red Auerbach was the new head coach for the 1950–'51 season.

Two key players who arrived that season were post player Ed Macauley and point guard Bob Cousy. Macauley was chosen in an NBA dispersal draft from the St. Louis Bombers. Cousy was selected in another dispersal draft from the Chicago Stags. Another fine addition was forward Chuck Cooper from Duquesne, whom Boston chose in the second round of the regular NBA draft. Another contributor was guard Sonny Hertzberg, a holdover from the previous season.

The Celtics, who played their home games in the Boston Arena during their first nine seasons, began the 1950–51 season with three road losses. They recovered quickly, though, and reeled off seven straight wins that were capped off by an 80–76 victory over the Bullets in Baltimore. It was an up-and-down season that resulted in a 39–30 record and second place in the Eastern Division. Macauley averaged 20.4 points and 9.1 rebounds per game, while Cousy averaged 15.6 points per game. The Celtics were swept, 2–0, by the New York Knicks in a first-round playoff series.

The next five seasons produced four winning records and five playoff berths with the help of other players such as Bill Sharman, Frank Ramsey, Don Barksdale, Jack Nichols, Jim Loscutoff, and Arnie Risen. Sharman arrived on April 26, 1951, in a trade with the Fort Wayne Pistons. Ramsey was a first-round draft pick in 1953 out of the University of Kentucky. Barksdale was traded from Baltimore on August 27, 1953, while Nichols was traded from the Milwaukee Hawks later that year on November 29. Loscutoff was a first-round draft pick in 1955 from the University of Oregon and Risen was sold by the Rochester Royals on October 26, 1955.

The 1956–57 season was when the winning truly began for Boston. The Celtics would capture 11 of the next 13 NBA championships. The pillar of that greatness was none other than Bill Russell. The huge center was acquired in a trade with St. Louis on April 30, 1956, after the Hawks chose him with the second overall pick in that day's NBA draft out of the University of San Francisco. "Bill Russell revolutionized NBA basketball," said Tom Heinsohn, another mainstay on those great Celtics teams. "He brought defense into the fore. He disrupted entire offenses. He was a fabulous shot blocker. During the course of his career, he became a more-than-effective offensive player." Heinsohn, a power forward, was taken in the 1956 draft out of the College of the Holy Cross as a territorial selection. Sam Jones, a forward-guard, arrived in 1957 when Boston selected him in the first round of the draft from North Carolina Central. K. C. Jones came aboard in 1958–59. The point guard had been a second-round draft pick in 1956 out of the University of San Francisco.

The remarkable list continues.

Arriving for the 1960–61 season was Tom "Satch" Sanders, a forward taken in the first round of the draft from New York University. John Havlicek came aboard in 1962–63, as did Larry Siegfried in 1963–64. Havlicek was a small forward-shooting guard whom the Celtics selected in the first round of the draft out of Ohio State. Siegfried was a rookie guard whom Boston signed as a free agent. Arriving in 1965–66 was Don Nelson, a forward who signed as a free agent. Coming aboard the next season was Bailey Howell, a veteran forward who was traded from the Baltimore Bullets.

"By the time I joined the Celtics," said Heinsohn, "Red had established a style of play with Bob Cousy, and they had perhaps the best backcourt in the league at the time with Cousy and Bill Sharman. They played up-tempo, fast-break basketball. Cousy even ended up the leading rebounder one year, and he was the point guard! That's what they needed to fuel the fast-break offense, and that's where Russell and I came in. Both of us were good rebounders, as was Jim Loscutoff, and Arnie Risen started at center. Russell missed about the first two months of the 1956–57 season because he was on the Olympic team. When he got back a few days before Christmas, he had to learn pro basketball, the physicality of it. Risen and Jack Nichols, another rebounder, really helped him in that regard. You could see that Bill had great potential as a rebounder to fuel the fast break."

By the time Russell returned from the Olympics, Boston was 16–8, with the help of a 10-game winning streak and had a three-game lead over the second-place Philadelphia Warriors in the Eastern Division. The Celtics finished 44–28 and won the East with relative ease. Sharman averaged 21.1 points per game and Cousy averaged 20.6.

The Celtics defeated the Syracuse Nationals three games to none in the East finals. Their opponent in the NBA Finals would be St. Louis. "The Hawks had some formidable players like Bob Pettit, Ed Macauley, and Slater Martin," said Heinsohn. Macauley had been traded by the Celtics to St. Louis as part of the Bill Russell trade. The Celtics trailed in the series, 1–0 and 2–1, but recovered to win their first championship four games to three in a hotly contested series. They won Game 7, 125–123, in double overtime at the Boston Garden. According to Heinsohn, "We had a nucleus of young players and older players, and I always maintained that that's the best combination where the young guys push the old ones and the old guys pull the young ones through. It's kind of a push-pull thing, and everything I've seen that's very competitive has had that dynamic."

The 1957–58 Celtics won their first 14 games and never looked back, finishing 49–23 and winning the East by eight games. They beat the Warriors four games to one in the division finals but, with Russell missing almost half of the series due to an injury, lost in six games to St. Louis for the league championship.

"After that, nobody touched us," said Heinsohn. "The next year, with K. C. Jones on the team, we had a full backup point-guard system and, along with Russell, we started to form one of the best defenses the league has ever seen. Really, it was the innovation of a defense that blocked shots and really took opponents out of their rhythm of what they wanted to do. The nucleus of the young players, Russell and myself, lasted until Cousy and Sharman retired and the Jones boys became the starting guards."

In 1958–59, eleven- and eight-game winning streaks helped Boston to a 52–20 record and the Eastern Division title by a dozen games over the New York Knicks. The Celtics beat Syracuse in seven games in the East finals before disposing of the Minneapolis Lakers, 4–0, for the NBA championship. "It was the first of many real battles we'd have with the Lakers on into their relocation to Los Angeles," said Heinsohn. "They had great players like Jerry West and Elgin Baylor. It was always a fun series when we played them."

The Celtics won the 1959–60 NBA championship by beating St. Louis in seven games for the title. In 1960–61, they defeated the Hawks again for the championship, this time in five games. The next season, Boston rolled to the East crown, finishing 60–20, 11 games over the second-place Warriors, who took the Celtics seven games before falling in the division finals. The Lakers, in their second season with Los Angeles as their home, was Boston's opponent in the NBA championship series. Said Heinsohn, "It went to the seventh game at the Boston Garden, and we all kind of held our breath when Frank Selvy had a chance to win it for LA, but missed a key shot. Russell grabbed the rebound, and the series was over. That was the closest they really came to beating us."

With Havlicek playing a key role, the Celtics beat the Lakers again, in six games, for the 1962–63 league title. "John is one of the all-time great Celtics players," Heinsohn said. "He was a very focused player. You wouldn't believe it, but he had two shots when he showed up as a rookie —a layup and a 15-foot runner. Bob Cousy made him a big-time player. Cousy was a long passer, and he would hit Havlicek right on the fingertips for layups. The next summer, John started to develop his game, and when he came back for his second season, he could dribble, he could hit the outside shot … he was a different player. He was the sixth man for several years while I was playing. He won a lot of games and was our go-to guy. He was a fabulous defensive player, too."

"John was a great player, one of the greats, no question about it," said Rick Barry.

In 1963–64, Boston began the season 7–0, got to 15–1, then 23–3, and won the East with a 59–21 record, but was challenged by the Cincinnati Royals, who finished just four games back. Havlicek averaged 19.9 points per game, Sam Jones averaged 19.4, and Russell put up 15 points and 24.7

rebounds per contest. The Celtics easily defeated the Royals, 4–1, in the East finals before knocking off the Warriors, who by then had moved to San Francisco, 4–1 in the NBA Finals. "That Warriors team had Wilt Chamberlain and Nate Thurmond, the original 'Twin Towers,'" Heinsohn recalled. "They couldn't beat us up the floor. We just outran them."

Did all the winning ever get boring? "No," said Heinsohn. "The guys the Celtics drafted were all very competitive people. Many had been part of successful teams in college—Cousy and myself at Holy Cross, Russell and K. C. Jones at San Francisco, Sharman at USC, and Havlicek at Ohio State. So that kind of resonated, and it carried over to the pros. Bill Russell and Bob Cousy both had this tremendous need to win, not that the others didn't, but these two guys were driven, and it carried over in a way that they were totally unselfish players. And that developed a team type of basketball. They weren't out to garner big numbers for themselves, they were out to garner big wins, and that's the way we approached it."

The 1964–65 Celtics finished 62–18 and won the East by 14 games. They defeated the Philadelphia 76ers, who, by way of a trade, had Chamberlain by then, in seven games—including a 110–109 win in Game 7 at the Boston Garden—for the East title. That Game 7 victory was clinched just seconds after Havlicek stole the ball off a Hal Greer inbounds pass, one of the most famous plays of all time. The Celtics then breezed past the Lakers in five games for yet another NBA title. The next season, with Nelson aboard, the Celtics were dethroned as regular-season East champions by the 76ers, whose 55–25 record was one game better than theirs. However, the Celtics easily dismantled the same Philadelphia team, four games to one, for the East crown. They beat the Lakers again in seven games for their eighth consecutive NBA championship.

"Before that 1965–66 season, Red called me and asked me my opinion of Nelson," recalled Heinsohn, who had retired after the previous season. "I said, 'He's slow as a turtle, Red, but he's one of two guys who I played against in the NBA who I could never get around. Everybody else I could get by. This guy, I could never get around him. He's a terrific rebounder and he's got a good jump shot.' And the Celtics ended up picking him up. He was a terrific offensive rebounder, especially in the late stages of games."

"Don wasn't the greatest athlete in the world but understood how to play the game," Rick Barry said. "He could shoot the ball, too."

Following the Celtics' championship in 1965–66, Auerbach retired from coaching and became the team's general manager. "Red offered me the head coaching job," said Heinsohn. "I told him I didn't think anybody could coach Russell but Russell himself. Red had such a unique relationship with a very proud guy in Bill Russell. I made the suggestion to Red that the guy who could probably get the most out of Russell because of his pride was Russell himself. I told him to make Russell the coach."

Auerbach heeded Heinsohn's advice and made Russell the Celtics' player-coach, making the Celtics the first major professional sports organization to hire a black management person.

Howell was a fine addition to the Celtics in 1966–67. "Bailey Howell was a guy who probably got as much out of his size and God-given natural ability than anyone," said Barry. "He could shoot the hook shot, he could take you in and post you up. He wasn't the most athletic guy in the world, but he'd get on the boards on the offensive glass. He was a heck of a player."

In 1966–67, Russell fared pretty darn well in his first season with dual responsibilities. He averaged 13.3 points and 21 rebounds per game. Sam Jones, Havlicek, and Howell each hung up at least 20 points per contest. Boston won 60 games but finished in second place in the East, eight games behind the 68–13 76ers, who defeated the Celtics, four games to one, for the East crown. Chamberlain and company went on to beat San Francisco for the league championship. In 1967–68, the Celtics finished 54–28 but again lost out to Philadelphia for the regular-season East title. However, after knocking off the Pistons, who had relocated to Detroit, 4–2, in the East semifinals, Boston recovered from a 3–1 series deficit to knock off Philadelphia in seven games for the East title. They then reclaimed the NBA championship by beating the Lakers in six games.

New to the team in 1968–69 was shooting guard Don Chaney, a first-round draft choice out of the University of Houston who would eventually become a very good player. "Don was a big guard, a tough guy," said Barry. "He played tough defense and was an intelligent player."

"Don was a fabulous athlete and probably the most coachable player I ever had," said Heinsohn, who would coach Chaney in the 1970s. "He was willing to learn, was a terrific rebounder for a guard, and a very good defensive player. He improved his game every year."

In 1968–69, the Celtics went 48–34 and fell to fourth place in the East. However, they got hot the last week of the regular season and carried that over into the playoffs. They easily defeated Philadelphia, minus Chamberlain, who had been traded to the Lakers, 4–1, in the East semifinals. They ousted the Knicks in six games for the East title before squeezing one last NBA championship from that era's magic bottle by beating the Lakers in seven games. With about 1:30 left in Game 7 at the Forum in Inglewood, California, Nelson's jumper from the foul line kicked high off the back rim and dropped straight through the basket, giving the Celtics a three-point cushion and catapulting them to a 108–106 victory. The result of the game embarrassed Lakers owner Jack Kent Cooke. Expecting a win, he had thousands of balloons with "World Champion Lakers" printed on them suspended from the rafters of the arena. As taken from an article posted on NBA.com on May 17, 2017, "Flyers were placed in every seat stating: 'When, not if, the Lakers win the title, balloons will be released from the rafters, the USC marching band will play Happy Days Are Here Again and broadcaster Chick Hearn will interview Elgin Baylor, Jerry West and Wilt Chamberlain in that order.'"

Russell retired. "He wanted to go out on top," said Heinsohn. "He reached a point where … he was playing 48 minutes practically every game. It was time for him to retire physically and emotionally. Sam Jones also retired." Auerbach hired Heinsohn to replace Russell as head coach for the 1969–70 season.

"We had to rebuild the basketball team," Heinsohn said.

Newcomers in 1969–70 were Jo Jo White and Steve Kuberski. White, a point guard, was a first-round draft pick. Kuberski was a fourth-round draft choice out of Bradley University. Also new to the team was veteran center Hank Finkel, who was acquired from the San Diego Rockets.

"Jo Jo came from the University of Kansas, and they weren't really playing up-tempo, fast-break basketball, Celtics style," said Heinsohn. "So he had to learn a whole new style of play, and he took to it like a duck to water. He loved to play basketball, was a fabulous competitor, and was a terrific athlete."

"Jo Jo was one of the great guards," said Barry. "He was an unbelievable offensive player. He could drive to the hoop and shoot from the outside.

He could score in any way. He was a heck of a player, one of the really outstanding players in the game."

"He was a complete player," Kuberski said. "You could see that he was going to be a good player."

"Steve was a guy who could play the power forward spot or the quick forward spot," Heinsohn said. "He could hit the outside shot and could rebound. He played effectively for us in his role."

Kuberski was a big fan of Heinsohn. "I liked Tommy," he said. "He was a player's coach. He just didn't want you to make mental mistakes and didn't want you to take bad shots. He didn't care if you missed a shot, he just wanted you to play hard and not make stupid mistakes and things like that."

The 1969–70 Celtics began the season terribly and never recovered. They lost their first four games and stood at 3–11 after a 113–98 loss at New York on November 15. They wound up 34–48 and in sixth place in the Eastern Division. It was the first time they failed to qualify for the postseason in 20 years.

"That first season without Bill Russell was a difficult adjustment," said Bob Ryan, who was in his first season as the Celtics beat writer for the *Boston Globe* and would continue on and off in that role for many years. "It was tough on Finkel, obviously a totally different species than Russell. They tried three centers. Heinsohn had a three-center committee of Finkel, Jim Barnes, and Rich Johnson. Havlicek responded with what was then the greatest year of his career. He led the team in scoring, rebounds, and assists. Nelson had a good year. Jo Jo and Kuberski showed promise, and Don Chaney was in his second year. They did beat the eventual league champion New York Knicks four out seven games. So there was a little hope, but they weren't physically equipped to compete with the better teams consistently. Everybody expected a tough year, and it *was* a tough year."

New to the Celtics in 1970–71 was center Dave Cowens, a first-round draft pick out of Florida State who was only 6-foot-9. "When Dave came in, that changed our whole team," said Kuberski. "At first, he was going to play forward, but then they decided to try him at center. And, boy, he took off from there. He was undersized, but he was a great athlete. He could do everything. He had a great outside shot he developed. You talk about a fierce competitor. I don't think I've ever seen anybody play as hard as Dave did.

"Cowens didn't start his first game at center. He started at forward, and Garfield Smith, another rookie, was who they thought would be the center," Ryan said. "After a while, Tommy switched Dave to center. There was a talk-show controversy in Boston about whether Cowens was too small to be a center. Well, he played much bigger than 6-9, and it didn't take long before he proved to people that he could play center. To this day, he's adamant about the fact that he loved playing center because it was the center of where all the action was. He was right in the middle of all the activity on offense and defense. You could throw the ball to him and he could make passes, and defensively he was great at directing people. He could really leap, too! He was aggressively strong and a born rebounder. Offensively, he had a good low-post power game and a decent, reliable face-up jumper, and he was very effective as a trailer on the fast break. He could run like hell. He could pitch the ball out and take off and get to the other end. He was so much fun to watch. He had Hall of Fame-level talent and an electrifying playing style."

"Dave was a mustang, a wild horse, who we corralled into a style of play," Heinsohn said. "He was tough-minded and wanted to win. He was the smallest center in the league, and we developed a style of play that they're using now in the NBA where we had a *point center*. He was handling the ball, and the Kareem Abdul-Jabbars and Bob Laniers and Wilt Chamberlains and Willis Reeds didn't know how to play him because we played him on the perimeter against those type of guys. The big guys hated to play him because he'd pull them out. That's the first time Wilt Chamberlain had to bend his knees to play defense on the perimeter. Against the smaller centers, we'd put Dave in the low post. So he could play two styles of basketball. He ended up being a prime ball handler in our no-center offense, which is kind of what's going on now with Golden State, the same concept. Dave changed the way the game was looked at and was the forerunner to today's game. He was a ferocious player. And, because of his coachability, we were able to play small basketball against big teams and win. We were able to accelerate the pace of the game.

"When he was in college, he was primarily a press center where he'd press after the ball was inbounded and then run back fast and press again, so he was a terrific athlete. But offensively he was not a big scorer in college, so we developed a system to bring out the offense. And he worked at it and became a terrific offensive player. He became a guy coming up behind the fast break and would make the jumpers outside. When he was learning the position, he'd miss a lot of those shots the first year, and he'd come over and say, 'I don't want to take these shots. I'm missing them.' And I told him, 'Dave, you're going to start making them sooner or later. And, when you start making them, they're gonna go crazy. You just keep shooting them. I'll tell you when to stop.' He was such an energetic player.

"We developed, with the smallest team in the league, a very, very up-tempo, aggressive style of offense, and coupled with a pressure type defense, we developed the ability to try to make people have to think super-fast running backwards and make quick decisions on the offense, and put guys who weren't used to handling the ball in difficult situations for them to make the proper pass. So everything was up-tempo, upbeat. People would come up to me and say, 'Don't these guys ever stop running?' And that's what we did. Cowens became a great player, Havlicek was just fantastic, and Jo Jo was an exemplary point guard. It was very effective because nobody else did it, and nobody else really had coordinated defenses to play against it."

"Cowens transformed the team," said Ryan. "That was the turning point in the fandom. He became an immediate fan favorite, so they started to draw a little bit better. Havlicek continued to play very well, and Jo Jo emerged and started to pay some dividends."

It was not enough, however, for the 1970–71 Celtics to qualify for the playoffs. They were inconsistent, but an early 10-game winning streak helped them to a 44–38 record, a 10-game improvement from the previous season, and third place in the new Atlantic Division of the new Eastern Conference. "But winning 44 games wasn't enough in the old playoff format," Ryan said.

According to Ryan, Heinsohn was a complicated coach. "When he was a rookie head coach, he'd lean on Red for some advice," he said. "He was coaching guys who, in some cases, he'd played with and, in one case, had been a roommate with in Havlicek. At the beginning, I think he did a lot of good things. He was an offensively oriented coach. His handling of Jo Jo became an issue. I think the veterans thought he was coddling him. They wanted Jo Jo to become more of a defensive player and a little more of a passer. But Tommy didn't want to mess up Jo Jo at all because his belief was, 'Jo Jo is scoring 20 points a game, and I don't want to mess him up,' like putting too much in his head. Some of the players started to get angry, so I think there was a problem there."

The 1971–72 Celtics, however, got off to a blazing 10–2 start, cooled off a bit, then rode the wave of ten- and nine-game winning streaks to a 56–26 record and first place in the Atlantic Division, eight games ahead of the second-place Knicks. Havlicek averaged 27.5 points per game, and White averaged 23.1. Cowens was a monster, netting 18.8 points and 15.2 rebounds per game. Boston defeated the Hawks, who had since relocated to Atlanta, four games to two, in the East semifinals, but were stopped cold in their tracks in losing to the Knicks, 4–1, in the East finals.

"That '71–'72 season," said Ryan, "was just a blossoming of Cowens having another great year, becoming one of the greatest players in the league, White feeling his way and starting to become a 20-point scorer, Chaney getting it down, and Kuberski making his contributions. Havlicek and Nelson continued their contributions, too. It was a disappointment losing to the Knicks, but it was a step forward year. The Knicks were in their prime. The Celtics couldn't handle Dave DeBusschere. That was the problem. They had a good matchup in the backcourt with Chaney and White against Walt Frazier and first Dick Barnett and then Earl Monroe, Havlicek and Bradley was a great matchup, and Cowens and Willis Reed was a great matchup, but DeBusschere was overwhelming. They couldn't handle him. He was their kryptonite. And if they couldn't get past the Knicks, they weren't going to the finals. That's why they needed Paul Silas."

And Paul Silas they got.

A veteran power forward, Silas was acquired by the Celtics in a trade with Phoenix. "That's what put them over the top and was the start of a terrific four-year run," Ryan said.

"Paul was the necessary ingredient we needed to really propel us to a level to play our type of game, the up-tempo game," said Heinsohn. "The one thing you need is rebounding, and he was a terrific rebounder. And our style of play enhanced his ability to rebound. And he could score. He was also a leader. He was such an important player. What he brought to the team was toughness, defense, and really a winning attitude. He ought to be in the Hall of Fame."

"Paul did all the dirty work—defense and rebounding, whatever you needed," said Kuberski.

The 1972–73 Celtics finished an astounding 68–14 and won the Atlantic Division by 11 games over New York. "They were the best team in the league," said Ryan. One player who showed flashes of brilliance but would not start coming into his own for a few years was guard Paul Westphal, a first-round draft pick in 1972 out of the University of Southern California.

"Our '72–'73 team, the smallest team in the league at the time, still has the record for best rebounding differential," Heinsohn said. "That's what we did. Everybody played every position. We had centers running in the middle of the floor as a middleman on the fast break, we had guards playing down in the low post at times. We never stopped moving. It was a different style of play. It was what I call offensive pressure basketball."

Boston beat Atlanta again, 4–2, in the East semifinals before a rematch with the Knicks for the East crown. But, in Game 3 at the Boston Garden, Havlicek got sandwiched in a pick between DeBusschere and Bradley and injured his right shoulder, causing him to miss the rest of that game and Game 4 at Madison Square Garden in New York. Recalled Ryan, "In Game 4, trailing two games to one, the Celtics had a 16-point lead going into the fourth quarter. Jake O'Donnell and Jack Madden turned in an atrociously refereed game and totally helped the Knicks get back in the game. This is not just my opinion; this is the universally shared viewpoint. Jack Kiser of the *Philadelphia Daily News* called it the 'Rape of Madison Square.'" The Celtics wound up losing, 117–110, in double overtime. "It was a bitter loss," said Ryan. "The Celtics did recover to win Games 5 and 6, forcing a Game 7 at Boston. We're all figuring the Celtics are going to win because, at that point in their history, they'd never lost a Game 7 at home, and they had all the momentum on their side. At the beginning of the game, the Knicks immediately swarmed all over Havlicek because he didn't have [use of] the right arm. He started turning the ball over." The Knicks won, 94–78.

The 1973–74 Celtics began the season 33–9, including twelve- and seven-game winning streaks. They put it in cruise control the rest of the way, finishing 56–26 and winning the Atlantic by seven games over the Knicks. "The second half of the season was real alarming," said Ryan. "We were a little worried going into the playoffs that the Celtics had lost their mojo. And in the first game of the first playoff series at home against Buffalo in the East semifinals, they were losing by 12 going into the fourth quarter. Then Cowens put on one of the great shows of his career. He had 20 points and nine rebounds in the fourth quarter alone, and the Celtics won the game. They went on to win in six games. The sixth game in Buffalo was quite exciting. With the game tied, Bob McAdoo blocked a shot by Jo Jo as time ran out. The referees gave White the benefit of the doubt and called the foul. White went to the line with no time left and made the two free throws to win the game. Afterwards, Paul Snyder, the owner of the Braves—I literally stood there and watched it—pounded on the door of the referees screaming, 'Mendy [Rudolph], the game was over!' He thought the play had happened after time had expired and that they should've gone to overtime. The Celtics went on to blow out the Knicks in five games in the conference finals. The Knicks were done. DeBusschere was hurt, and Reed was on his last legs."

Boston's opponent in the NBA Finals was Kareem Abdul-Jabbar and the Milwaukee Bucks. "Milwaukee played handicapped the whole series," Ryan recalled. "They'd lost Lucius Allen prior to the series. He got hurt in a bizarre accident when he slipped on a warmup jacket left along the sidelines in the previous series against Chicago. He was a starting guard, a speedy guard, and they didn't have him. Then Jon McGlocklin got hurt in the first game of the finals. So they wound up with a backcourt of Oscar Robertson, who was on his last legs, and Mickey Davis, who normally played small forward."

Said Ryan, "With the Celtics up three games to two in Game 6 at the Garden, they were down late, and then Cowens made that famous play. He knocked the ball away from Oscar, dove for it, and the Bucks were called for a 24-second violation. I think, at that point, Cowens was 4-for-17 from the floor. He hit a jump shot to force overtime. In the second overtime, Havlicek scored nine points and looked like he was going to be the hero when Boston had the lead. Then Kareem threw in a 17-foot hook from the right baseline. Only Kareem could do that. And the Bucks won the game by one point."

"We were kind of dejected that we had to go play at Milwaukee [two days later] on Sunday afternoon," Heinsohn said.

The Celtics, though, got off to a great start. "Cowens made up for his bad performance overall in Game 6," said Ryan. "He had a big first half when I think he had eight field goals. He was hitting his outside shot. Oscar Robertson was 35 years old and, again, on his last legs. He couldn't handle Chaney. Chaney was all over him. He didn't have the legs to come back after playing Friday night. The decision had been made after Game 6 in a powwow in Red's office that, for the first and only time, they would double-team and triple-team Kareem. They'd always let Cowens guard him by himself, but they were going to surprise Kareem and make somebody else beat them."

"There wasn't a lot of double-teaming because there wasn't a three-point play and things didn't get spread out, so it wasn't that efficient," Cowens said on the *Legends with Leyden* show on Fox News 25 in Boston. "For my first four years and the first six games in the finals, it was me against Jabbar, and we were doing okay. I mean, it was 3–3 at the time. It wasn't like what we were doing wasn't working. But [the switch] really made them think. It surprised them. Because they couldn't get the ball to Jabbar in enough time to utilize the shot clock, it put them in a little bit of a panic, and we got out to a lead and were able to keep that lead. It helped in the beginning of that game. We made the change and never practiced it. We didn't even have a shootaround or anything. We just talked about it. A team that was together as long as we'd been, with that experience we didn't have to practice. We knew what to do."

Said Ryan, "Jabbar was held scoreless for a long, long stretch in the second and third quarters, at which point the Celtics got up by 17."

"I'd played in so many seventh games that I knew that the crowd was very important," Heinsohn said. "I was searching for a way to keep the crowd out of the game and hope for us to get off to a good start. So we came out and pressured the Milwaukee guards, disorganized their offense by making them work the ball up the floor, and we cut off as much as possible angles of passes to Kareem. And it worked. We totally caught Milwaukee by surprise."

"You knew Milwaukee was going to come back, though, and they did," said Ryan. "They got it down to three, and that's when Paul Westphal made the big play of the game. He drove baseline and made a beautiful left-handed reverse shot that started the Celtics back on the path. Then Havlicek up-faked at the free throw line, drove through the lane, hit a shot and got fouled, and made a three-point play." The Celtics went on to win, 102–87. They were NBA champions for the first time since Bill Russell's final season in 1968–69.

"That was a very stirring finals."

"It was a unique series in that each team won significant games on the road," said Heinsohn.

Cowens broke his foot during the 1974–75 exhibition schedule, causing him to miss the first 17 games of the regular season. The Celtics certainly missed him. They went 9–8 in his absence. Soon after his return, they dominated. At one point, they won 18 of 19 games en route to a 60–22 record and first place in the Atlantic by 11 games over second-place Buffalo. Three newcomers who provided bench help were Jim Ard, Glenn McDonald, and Kevin Stacom. Ard, a center, was signed as a free agent. A small forward, McDonald was a first-round draft selection out of Long Beach State. Stacom was a second-round draft pick from Providence College.

"Ard played really well in Cowens's place early in the season," said Ryan.

"Jim was fast and could shoot it, and he rebounded," Heinsohn said.

"Jim was a big, strong individual," added McDonald. "He'd take it to the boards. When you needed a rebound, he'd get it for you. He also had a nice short jump shot."

"Glenn was a great talent," said Kuberski. "He could run, jump, and shoot."

"He was very dedicated to the game," Ard added. "He kept himself in shape, looking for the break to get in the games and play."

"Stacom was an excellent jump shooter and a good athlete going up and down the floor," said Ryan. "He was hardworking and smart. He got as much out of his ability as he could."

"Kevin was a guy who came off the bench and really would play aggressive, physical defense against the point guards," Heinsohn said. "He could score, too. He was an effective player."

Boston easily beat the Houston Rockets, four games to one, in the East semifinals. Next up in the conference finals were Elvin Hayes, Wes Unseld, and the Washington Bullets, who also were 60–22 during the regular season. The Celtics had a 12-point lead at halftime of Game 1 at the Boston Garden, but wound up losing, 100–95. "They never got it back," said Ryan. "Losing Game 1 at home was the key. They were playing catchup the rest of the way and eventually lost in six games. They lost fair and square. No argument. They got beat, and that was that."

THE '75-'76 SUNS

There were many new faces on the Phoenix Suns in 1975–76. One was center Alvan Adams, a first-round draft pick from the University of Oklahoma, where he had played under John MacLeod his freshman year. "Heading into my first training camp with the Suns," said Adams, "I was thinking to myself, 'How much can John help me or coddle me?' But he had to make sure that it was just the opposite. He couldn't be showing any favoritism to the guy he'd been recruiting since ninth grade. And he told me, 'I'm gonna work you hard, I can't show any favoritism.' I go, 'I understand. I understand completely.'"

According to Adams, MacLeod was a fair coach but ran a grueling training camp. "He worked us all hard," he said. "We worked on the basics every day in training camp. We scrimmaged hard. He prepped us. He warned me of a lot of stuff. He said, 'Alvan, you need to get your rest. Don't be out running around. I know you're a curious guy, but you can't be walking around downtown historic Prescott, Arizona, looking at the architecture. The first road trip, you can't be walking around looking at every newspaper stand in the airport. You've got to conserve your energy. It's 82 games plus eight preseason games. That's three years in college.' I go, 'Okay, okay, okay.' But, of course, I was young. I still wandered around the airport carrying team equipment because I was the rookie. You worked hard, and you got to jump in the pool after practice because you lived in Arizona. And I loved it."

"True story," recalled Keith Erickson in the *Boston Globe*. "First trip to New York. We're riding in on the bus, and it's a classic traffic crawl. Alvan is looking out at the tall buildings and the traffic, and he just comes out with 'Gol-lee!' It was exactly what you'd expect this kid from Oklahoma to say."

MacLeod told Adams that he would be playing backup forward and backup center. He had to win the starting center position from Dennis Awtrey. "Who do we play in our very first preseason game?" Adams remembered. "The Lakers and their new center, Kareem Abdul-Jabbar, at the University of California at Santa Barbara. I had number 33 because, when I got to junior high school, they asked me what number I wanted. I said, 'Well, 33 because the greatest center is Lew Alcindor [Abdul-Jabbar's given name] at UCLA, and I want his number on my uniform.' And they said, 'We only go to 15.' I go, 'All right, I'll take 11.' Then, in high school, they asked me what number I wanted. I said, '33.' They go, 'Yep.' Dennis got injured and couldn't play against the Lakers. John said, 'Alvan, you're starting at center.' I'd run my big toenail off in training camp. We cut a hole in my shoe to take the pressure off my toe, so my right big toe stuck out. I was shaking Kareem's hand before the opening tip, and I felt like saying, 'Mr. Jabbar, can you please not step on my right big toe in this game?'

"This was the first NBA game I ever saw live. I was eager and ready to play. I was conditioned to prepare for the game and be even keeled and not get too up or too down for any one game, but yikes! This was the first game. The toe hurt for a while, but as I started running more, it felt fine. I don't remember who won, but I'm pressing full court, I'm running up and down the court, outrunning Kareem. I'm a quick, big guy, so I was at the front of the press. I do recall we made a basket, and Kareem took the ball out of bounds, and I pressured and stole the pass and went up and made a layup or a dunk. And one of my teammates said to me, 'Don't get Kareem upset in the preseason.' I remember being pleased with my performance, thinking, *I can play in this league. Who's next?*

"I remember thinking to myself, *Basketball's basketball. Wow! I'm getting a chance to play with the best in the world.* I never got too confident because John always kept us on an even keel, telling us, 'If you win a game, that's great, but we have another game in two nights' and 'You got dunked on, don't worry about it, get to the next play' and 'You made a great play, get back on defense.' He told us to stay healthy, stay rested, stay hydrated, eat well, listen, run the plays, that it's a team game, not an individual game."

Another newcomer to Phoenix in 1975–76 who praised Adams was Paul Westphal, whom the Suns acquired in a trade with Boston in which the Celtics received All-Star guard Charlie Scott as part of the deal. "Paul and I were on the phone during the '75–'76 exhibition season," recalled Bob Ryan, "and he says to me, 'We have here a young man [Adams] who can play basketball.' Alvan was all about finesse. He may have been the personification of a finesse kind of ballplayer of all time. He was a great passer, a fearless passer. He'd try and squeeze bounce passes through traffic, probably to the detriment of his team, in the last minute of a tie game. He was a good shooter with good range and was a good player. He was a smart player and a good defensive player."

"Alvan was undersized but very, very athletic," said John Wetzel, who was back with the Suns after spending three seasons with the Atlanta Hawks. "He could shoot the ball from around the free throw line, maybe from 17 feet. He could run like a deer. He'd outrun guys at his position and get a lot of easy baskets just simply because he could run. He out-quicked a lot of the big guys who had to guard him."

"He was tremendously talented," added Awtrey, who wound up losing his starting spot to Adams. "He just made things look easy. He made it by his wits and by his talent."

"Alvan got the most out of his abilities," said Rick Barry.

"Dennis was a perfect backup to Alvan," Jerry Colangelo said. "He gave us a different look. Dennis was bigger and stronger and had a different game than Alvan. He was a good fit for our roster and an excellent backup center for us at that time."

As for Westphal, he will likely go down as one of the smartest players in the history of the NBA.

"We had a very talented player in Charlie Scott but came to a decision that it would be best to move forward," said Jerry Colangelo. "In checking the marketplace, there was the possibility of acquiring Paul Westphal, who was a young player sitting on the bench in Boston. We felt his great potential would be a target, and so that trade took place. And he, given the opportunity to blossom, developed into an All-League performer."

"I could see pros and cons of the trade," Westphal said. "I wasn't expecting to get traded, so it was a surprise. I was really looking forward to the next season playing with the Celtics because I loved playing with them. I was envisioning myself playing my whole career there. So it was a huge disappointment in that regard, going from a team that had championship aspirations every year to a team that hadn't been very good in the Suns. But, at the same time, it was a great opportunity, and moving west and having been raised in Southern California and being closer to home, I considered that a plus even though I loved Boston. It was a new opportunity that took some getting used to."

"Paul was my favorite teammate of all time," said Adams. "He knew where I was, and I knew where he was on the court. I'd run down the court, he'd throw it to me, I'd catch it, I'd score. He'd run down the court, I'd throw it to him, he'd catch it, he'd score. We were runners, we could pass the ball, we could catch it. We had a very productive partnership."

"Paul was really a good player. He was a talented guy," Wetzel said. "He could handle the ball, could pass the ball, and really could get to the basket. He had a great first step getting by his defender. He could finish at the basket with either hand. When he came to Phoenix, it really upgraded the team."

"If I had somebody bringing the ball up the court one-on-one, who would I want to be the guy? I would've picked Paul Westphal," said Awtrey. "He could shoot outside, he could shoot inside, left-handed, right-handed, he was creative. He was about as good offensively as anybody that I saw play in those days."

"Paul was one of the truly outstanding guards in the game," said Barry.

Three other players who arrived on the scene in 1975–76 were John Shumate and reserves Phil Lumpkin and Pat Riley. Shumate, a power forward, had been a first-round draft pick in 1974 out of Notre Dame. Lumpkin, a guard, was acquired in a trade with the Portland Trail Blazers. A veteran guard, Riley was traded from the Lakers.

"John was a real springy jumper," said Adams. "He was always on his toes, he could score, he was a good rebounder, and he was a good defender. He was a good all-around player. He was a real talent."

"He needed the ball. If he got the ball low, it was really hard to stop him," said Awtrey. "He had good size, he was strong, and he knew how to use his body very well. Phil was kind of a smooth player. He knew how to play basketball. He distributed the ball well. If you were open, he'd get the ball to you."

"Phil didn't play that much, but when he'd come in, he always settled the team down and knew exactly what John [MacLeod] wanted him to do. He just fit in perfectly," said Al Bianchi, who didn't join the team until late January when the American Basketball Association's Virginia Squires, for whom he was the head coach, were sold.

"Pat was a very important part of that team," said Westphal. "He, along with Keith Erickson, had been on Lakers teams that were championship contenders and won the whole thing in 1972. Both he and Keith had a lot of stories about what it took to win in the league. Pat and Keith both were really good veterans for us."

Shumate said that Riley knew how to play the game and that he was a good teammate on the bench. He remembers sitting next to Riley and said that he would point things out to him and tell him what was going wrong and the adjustments he needed to make.

Phoenix's starting lineup at the beginning of the 1975–76 season had Westphal and Dick Van Arsdale as the guards, Adams as the center, and Shumate and Curtis Perry as the forwards. The Suns were challenged right off the bat—by the schedule makers. Their first six games were on the road. They won two of them, 89–88 over Portland in the opener and 96–80 over Chicago in their fourth game. They heated up a little and, after a five-point home win over Milwaukee on December 17, stood at 14–9. But, beginning with a 128–124 double-overtime loss at home to Cleveland two nights later, things began to unravel. They lost 18 of their next 22 games, including a 105–96 loss to the Bucks on January 29 that dropped their record to 18–27. Two night later, the Suns beat Philadelphia, but the damage had been done. They were sinking fast and, with the All-Star break ahead, realized they needed help, some sort of spark to get the season headed in the right direction again.

As for the All-Star Game, which was played on February 3 at The Spectrum in Philadelphia, Phoenix's lone representative was Adams. "That was the first big awakening for me," he said, "making the All-Star team. I was like, 'What? I'm an All-Star? Wow! It wasn't that long ago that I was on a college team not even able to make it to the NIT [National Invitation

Tournament]!" Backing up Kareem Abdul-Jabbar, Adams scored four points and had three rebounds in the Western Conference's 123–109 loss to the Eastern Conference.

Two days earlier, on February 1, the spark that the Suns needed, Colangelo and MacLeod hoped, arrived by way of a trade that, as part of the deal, sent Shumate to Buffalo. His name was Gar Heard. He was a veteran power forward. In 50 games with the Braves that season, he averaged 9.9 points and 10.2 rebounds per game.

Shumate said that it was a sad day in his life when MacLeod called him to tell him that he had been traded to Buffalo. In 43 games for the Suns that season, he averaged 11.3 points and 5.6 rebounds per game. He said the weather in Phoenix the day he was traded was 90 degrees, but when he arrived in Buffalo the next day it was about 90 degrees *below zero* with the wind-chill factor. He said he missed everything about the Suns experience.

"I'd heard a rumor that I was going to be traded during the All-Star break, but I never thought it would be Phoenix. I thought it would be Los Angeles," Heard said. "I was home in Atlanta during the All-Star break, and I got the call from Rudy Martzke, Buffalo's public relations guy, telling me that I'd been traded. So I said, 'Okay, where? LA?' He said, 'No, close. You're going to Phoenix.' I kind of hesitated a little bit because I was going from a team that was 30–20 to a team that was 19–27. I said to myself, *Okay, there go the playoffs.* Then John called me the same night and said, 'Hey, I want you here, and I finally got you, so I want you to come out here, and we're going to be all right. You're the piece that I need to bring this team together. Everyone is going to get healthy.'"

"Gar had played for John at Oklahoma," said Colangelo. "So John knew him well, knew his strengths and weaknesses. He brought experience to our team, and he fit in immediately."

"He came in and gave us, because we were undersized with Alvan at center, a little more rebounding to go with Curtis Perry," said Bianchi.

"Gar turned us around," said Awtrey. "He settled the team down."

"Gar and Curtis would be classified as power forwards, but they both had the ability to hit perimeter shots also," Colangelo said. "It just really depended on who we had on the floor at what time. Alvan was a guy, with his height and weight, playing against the big centers in the league …

he was a high-post center, so that gave guys like Perry and Heard the opportunity to do some post-up offensively."

"John Shumate was a very talented low-post player," added Westphal. "It's kind of an unfair rap on him, but it seemed like, when he was traded for Gar, the chemistry worked."

Phoenix's first game after the All-Star break was on February 6 at home against the defending NBA champion—and Pacific Division rival—Golden State Warriors, who had since relocated across the San Francisco Bay to Oakland. Behind Heard's 17 points, 13 rebounds, and five assists, the Suns defeated the Warriors, 118–111.

"Once we acquired Heard, we started to play good, solid basketball, and it just started to build and grow," said Colangelo.

The Suns won two more games, lost one, won one, and lost two, and carried a 23–30 record into a game at New Orleans on February 20. This is when a negative turned into a positive and is what really turned the season around. Early in the game, Van Arsdale was undercut and broke his wrist. Replacing him was Rookie Ricky Sobers, whom the Suns selected in the first round of the 1975 NBA draft out of UNLV. Sobers went on to score eight points and help the Suns to a 103–102 victory over the Jazz.

"We were on our way to the airport the next day to fly to Houston, and the club was down because Dick was going to be sent back to Phoenix," remembered Al McCoy. "Coach MacLeod had the bus driver stop the bus and pull off the freeway. MacLeod went to every player and said, 'I know everybody's down because we don't know when Dick Van will be back, but we've got to put it together because we're going to make the playoffs.' He issued them a challenge of what they wanted to do. Did they want to win? Did they want to forget the season? Were they going to feel sorry for themselves? And they all stood up and said, 'We want to win.' That day seemed to turn these guys around, and they were young players for the most part. They got fired up. The way Coach MacLeod handled it was great, and the guys responded to it. The attitude picked up, the intensity picked up, and the energy reached a high for the year."

"Ricky gave us some toughness," Bianchi said. "He was a little bit headstrong, but we liked that. Eventually, he fit right in."

"He was a real leader on the floor, but his toughness, his defense, and his ability to knock down perimeter shots made him very valuable to us," said Colangelo. "There really wasn't a legitimate point guard. Ricky and Paul were guards. Dick's injury gave Sobers an opportunity, and once he got that opportunity, it was hard to get him out of the lineup. He had earned that starting spot."

The Suns began playing better basketball. By March 18, they were 32–36 with postseason dreams dancing in their heads. A 106–100 home win over the Pistons that night fueled a seven-game winning streak that upped their record to 39–36 and set them up for a serious run at the playoffs.

"We just built confidence during the second half of the season, and we felt we could compete," said Colangelo. "We had no idea what that really meant at the time. I think it was a matter of slowly gaining confidence during the course of the second half of the season in building momentum."

Phoenix clinched a berth in the postseason on April 8 by defeating the Lakers at home, 113–98, behind Sobers's 23 points and six assists.

"We just barely eked into the playoffs," said Wetzel.

Phoenix finished with a 42–40 record and in third place in the Pacific Division, a game behind second-place Seattle and miles behind first-place Golden State, which wound up a league-best 59–23.

Westphal averaged 20.5 points and 5.4 assists per game. Adams averaged 19 points, 9.1 rebounds, and 5.6 assists per game and was named NBA Rookie of the Year.

"Westphal was probably one of the best offensive players then and now and for a long time," said Bianchi. "He was very athletic and had a very good mind offensively. If you want big-fire guys in the crucial situation who you want to take the shot, I'll take him. He was one of those guys who was tuned in all the time."

Shumate said that Westphal always played with a little smile on his face and that he was very deceptive. He said that he would take guys off the dribble, go to the basket, and dunk the ball. He said that he had a great pull-up jumper and was ambidextrous also. He said he was very smart and had a high basketball IQ and a tremendous feel for the game, especially on the offensive end of the floor.

"He could get a shot off in a snowstorm," said Perry. "He was a very effective and crafty offensive player. He had a really good feel for the game."

"Paul could do just about anything offensively," said Van Arsdale.

"He was also tough. He was a hard-nosed dude," Fred Saunders said. Shumate added that he feared nobody.

"Alvan was terrific," said Bianchi. "He could run, he was smart, and when it comes to all-time passing centers, he's probably at the top of the list. He was just incredible."

"He really didn't have any weaknesses," Westphal said. "He was unselfish, he could shoot the ball with either hand, he was fundamentally as sound as you get, and he wasn't afraid to make plays. If he thought you were open, he'd throw the ball to you. He never hesitated to take the play that he saw. He was a very smart player."

Added Perry, "Alvan was maybe a little light for the center position, but he used his skills as a perimeter player and could drive to the basket."

Shumate said the thing that really amazed one about Adams was that, even with all the big-name players like Kareem Abdul-Jabbar and Elvin Hayes, one just thought that this tall, skinny kid was in trouble and was going to get destroyed. He said that Adams did not get destroyed because he was exceptionally smart, and he was one of those guys who could transfer his intellectual smartness from the classroom onto the basketball court. Shumate said Adams had a tremendous offensive feel for the game and that he was a highly deceptive athlete. He said that he would drive on guys like Abdul-Jabbar and Hayes and take them out and shoot the ball or he would fake the shot and then drive to the basket and dunk. He said it was just amazing. He added that Adams had a tremendous repertoire of shots using both hands. He said he was a phenom.

"The combination of Westphal and Adams just matured to the point where they were like a hand in a glove," said Erickson. "They knew *exactly* what the other guy was going to do, and they both played exceptionally well toward the end of the season."

Perry and Heard were monsters underneath in 1975–76. Perry averaged 13.3 points and 9.6 rebounds per game. In 36 games with the Suns, Heard hung up 12.4 points and 9.9 boards per contest.

"I loved Curtis," said Adams. "Me being an undersized center, I relied a lot on him. He was a great rebounder. He was so important to our success. With he and Gar on the front line, I could afford to front a guy like Kareem because I knew we had the veteran weak-side help to lend some resistance. It was a really effective front line with a rookie center."

"Curtis wasn't a primary scorer, but he had his moments where he could score quite well," Wetzel said. "He was a pretty smooth player, knew how to play, and had a good feel for the game."

"I don't think he got enough credit for what he did with the Suns," said Heard. "He could guard almost anybody. Most of the time, he guarded the scorer on the other team. He was a very aggressive guy, a good rebounder. He was kind of the glue that put the team together."

Shumate said that Perry was one of the grandpapas of the team. He said that, if one was headed in the wrong direction, not doing what one was supposed to be doing, or was late for practice, he would pull that player aside have a talk with him. He said that Perry was always the mother hen, the old pro, who always was looking out for the rookies, especially to make sure that they stayed focused and were headed in the right direction. He said he was a tough guy.

"Perry was a solid, industrious forward. He was never an All-Star but was a pro's pro," Bob Ryan added.

"Gar really was the missing piece to our late-season success to get into the playoffs," said Adams. "He was a rugged rebounder. He held the ball high and had a high arc on his jump shots. He was a good shot blocker, too."

"He was the big dog," Perry said. "He was the missing piece to what we needed as far as making other teams adjust to the way we played. His defensive prowess with blocking shots and steals was very good. He was a smart player."

"Gar could play in the post and guard the post but was still agile enough to be able to defend smaller players as well. He could score a little, too," said Westphal.

Added Awtrey, "Gar wasn't a great shooter, but he'd knock it down when he needed to."

"He adapted early to the Suns and was a huge, huge contributor," McCoy said.

Van Arsdale, who returned from his injury on April 3, averaged 12.9 points per game in 1975–76. Erickson netted 10.1 points per contest.

"Dick Van Arsdale was one of the toughest competitors who I ever played with," said Wetzel. "He was just a tough guy. He could score, had a tremendous ability to get to the basket, had that body where he could create contact, and would shoot a lot of free throws because of that."

"He'd do anything you wanted him to do," said Bianchi. "He worked hard, he got after people, and he could shoot the ball a little bit."

"Dick worked hard in practice," Adams said. "He'd go driving right through a brick wall if he needed to get a basket. He was critical to us."

"We looked at Dick as the stable force," said Heard. "He was a veteran who'd been around a long time. He was a solid guy, a strong guy, the guy we all looked up to."

"Dick was a consummate professional," Westphal said.

Added Perry, "He took pride in being 'The Original Sun.'"

"Keith could do a lot of things," said Bianchi. "He could guard, he could rebound, he could run. When he had good games, we were really good."

"He wasn't going to jump and dunk on people, he was just smooth," Adams said. "He could knock down shots, though, and be in the right place at the right time."

"Keith was a veteran with a lot of savvy and a lot of moxie," said Wetzel. "He really knew how to play. He was one of the guys who'd come off the bench, play a lot of minutes, and was very effective,"

Also in 1975–76, Sobers averaged 9.2 points per game.

"Ricky was like an enforcer. He was a tough guy," said Heard. "When he became our starting point guard, he kind of took the pressure off Westphal because Paul didn't have to handle the ball as much. It freed him up to score a lot more. Ricky kind of set the tone for the guards."

"Ricky was tough as nails," Perry said. "There was no backdown in him. He took up the challenge for whatever the task called for. He guarded people, he scored, he passed the ball, he ran the offense—as a rookie! His task was to make sure that we ran John's offense, which was very effective, and he made use of the talents of the guys who were out on the floor with him."

"There was just something about Ricky … he played with somewhere between arrogance and swagger, confidence, a tough, tough guy," said Ryan. "It was like he was never a rookie. He walked in and said, 'Fuck you, guys.' He was a handful but also poised."

"Anytime there was a scrum or a melee on the floor, he'd be in the middle of it," Wetzel added.

Said Saunders, "Ricky played with a chip on his shoulder and wanted to make sure he got his due."

The rest of the reserves on the 1975–76 Suns knew their jobs, did them well, and never complained about lack of playing time.

"Dennis Awtrey was the opposite of Alvan, who was a finesse guy," said Wetzel. "Dennis was the brute and the brawn. He'd come in and bang guys and take a hard foul. He was very effective. He'd play hurt, too, and never complain when he had a sprained ankle or a banged-up knee."

"Dennis was a very professional center," Westphal said. "He wasn't the most talented guy, but he was smart and knew his limitations. He was probably one of the best backup centers of his era."

"Nate Hawthorne was a good spot guy. He was effective," said Awtrey. "He jumped well, he shot the ball decently, and was a good all-around player."

"Nate was a good leaper, kind of springy," said Wetzel.

Added McCoy, "He came off the bench and provided some spark."

"Pat Riley didn't play that much, but when he did, he always seemed to contribute," Bianchi said. "He just did his job."

"I remember Pat being very serious and very studious and very much a professional. I learned a lot from him," said Adams.

"Phil Lumpkin was a good player," said Saunders. "He didn't have superior speed, but he had a good, little spacing game and could shoot if he got open."

Shumate said that he was a good, everyday workmanlike player.

"Mike Bantom was a good player," said Awtrey. "He could shoot the ball a little bit and was a good rebounder."

"He was a talented, young forward," added Westphal.

"Fred Saunders was strong, he was quick as could be, he could jump like crazy, and he could run like a deer," said Erickson. "It was terrible to have to guard him in practice. I have no idea why he wasn't playing all the time because he was such an incredible physical talent. At times, we'd be scrimmaging, and I'd be guarding him, and some of my smart-aleck teammates would be laughing at me because I just couldn't do anything with this Fred Saunders. He was so quick and so good. And when he was hot, you just couldn't do anything."

"John Wetzel was smart. He could do a little bit of everything," Awtrey said. "He played decent defense and had good size."

"He was very studious," said Adams. "He practiced hard, he pushed the guys in practice, and he made Paul and Ricky better."

"John didn't get a lot of minutes," Perry said, "but he was ready when they called for him."

As for John MacLeod, he got nothing but rave reviews from his players and his superiors. "John was the perfect head coach for that team," said Westphal. "He was a great teacher, and he believed strongly in team play, fundamentals, and repetition. He never really seemed to get down. He'd always come back to practice after whatever happened the day before with an attitude that whatever's ahead, we're going to meet that challenge. He was just an excellent coach."

"Once John got a feel for it and a little bit better talent to work with, he did a terrific job," Colangelo said.

"John was always prepared and always prepared us," said Adams. "He always stressed the basics; he was always positive. I listened to him not just because he was the coach but because I believed that he knew what he was doing. He had us believing that any game we went into we could win because we worked hard in practice. He always stressed that you only play as well in a game as you practice the day before, and I subscribed to that, too, and still do today, that the results will come if you put the work in."

"I have great respect for John. He was an excellent coach," Wetzel said. "He had a game plan and knew what he wanted to get done. He stuck to his guns in what he thought was right. The players played hard for him. He was a demanding coach, didn't put up with any nonsense. If the bus leaves at six, the bus leaves at six. If you're there one minute after six, you're likely going to be left behind. He had rules and he stuck by them. He was disciplined and, for that '75–'76 team, he was a good coach. That team needed direction. We didn't have any superstars, and we played together, we played the right way, we worked hard in practice, and we defended as best we could."

Said Ryan, "I always marveled at how MacLeod managed to distribute minutes. He was amazing that way. He used his bench very well. He was a damn good coach."

"John MacLeod was one of the finest coaches I ever had the opportunity to work with," McCoy added. "He was a brilliant statistician. He was a great down-to-the-earth basketball coach."

Shumate said that MacLeod was very tough and had a lot of grit. He said he was really smart and an outstanding basketball man and that he was a fabulous teacher and lecturer, too.

"He was a down and dirty guy, just keep working hard no matter what, that kind of a guy," said Erickson.

"Believe it or not, I really wasn't that fond of John in college," Heard said. "At Oklahoma, he wanted everything to be slow pace, pass the ball four or five times. He put a lot of emphasis on defense and rebounding. That was his thing. But that helped me out in my pro career because, even though I didn't score as much, I became a much better defensive player and a much better rebounder in college."

As for Al Bianchi, he brought a wealth of professional coaching experience to the table. "He was a perfect fit for John, who had limited NBA experience. He was a valuable asset to him," said Colangelo.

"John was only a few years out of college coaching, and sometimes he hinted more towards the college type of thing," said Awtrey. "Al relaxed him a little bit and cleaned up some things. They made a good team together. I think they were both better by being with each other."

"Al would let his emotions get in the way sometimes with the referees," Wetzel said. "He had fire in his belly. Coaching was an extension of him as a player [he played 10 years in the 1950s and 1960s with the Syracuse Nationals and Philadelphia 76ers]. He was a really intense guy. He had a good basketball mind, too, and had a good head on his shoulders."

Shumate said that Bianchi was hard-nosed and took no crap from anyone. He said he was a tough guy.

Colangelo should not be forgotten, either. He is the one who put the 1975–76 Suns together. "Jerry really understood basketball," Awtrey said. "One of the things I really liked about him was, when things were going bad, he took all the pressure off the coach and said, 'Look at me.' When things started going good he said, 'Look at John.' He took the criticism, and when the praise came, he pushed it off onto other people. I really respected him for that."

According to Bianchi, the Suns were a low-maintenance team. "The players all got along well, there was never any upheaval, and the chemistry was really good," he said. "John did a magnificent job of putting guys in their places and substituting. I can't stress how important that was. The players were regimented like John was. They were schooled, and they were programmed. They knew what to do. The guy coming in knew what to do. You have to have those kinds of people because they buy into it. And the coach can't do anything unless they do what you want them to do.

"With that kind of team, everybody is feeling good, even reserves like Erickson, Wetzel, Lumpkin, and Riley. We had help from a lot of people. We got on a roll and, once we got on that roll, boy, the team was playing well. Gar was another low-maintenance guy, and the trade that brought him to Phoenix started it. When a team catches fire like that, that's when you want it—at the end of the year."

"You've got to have some chemistry out there, guys playing together for a while and getting things cooking," said Perry. "After Gar got there, we had practice time. John liked his practices. You get to run through stuff, and you get a feel for your teammates' strengths and where you can be most effective. We had the third-best record in the league after the All-Star break."

"We had veterans who'd had a lot of success when you look at Keith and Pat with Los Angeles and Curtis with Milwaukee," said Westphal. "Dick had been an All-Star several times. Dennis had been a part of the Chicago Bulls teams that were really good. I'd been on successful Celtics teams, even though I didn't play that much, especially my first year. So we felt like we had enough experience. A lot of us just expected that we were going to have a good team if we were healthy. And John certainly expected we'd be good if we were healthy. We were fighting injuries a lot the first part of the year. It seemed like everything came together, and I don't think any of us stopped believing that we had a good team. We just had to go out and prove it."

"After a while, we believed that we could beat anybody, especially at home. And that's the way we finished the season," Heard said. "We felt that we were one of the best teams in the league. We felt that we were never out of a ballgame."

Said Erickson, "It was a combination of having confidence in Paul, particularly being able to score almost at will with the help of Alvan and his great passing, and Gar, Curtis, and Ricky being as tough as nails defensively. We were just a really good team. We all played together really well."

Shumate said that one thing that team had was tremendous character.

"We were a much better team at the end of the season than we were at the start," Awtrey said. "We may have only been 42–40, but we finished strong. It's nice when you're going to the playoffs, and you take a look at the team and see that you're more well balanced than you were at the beginning of the season. We had some guards who could shoot the ball. Ricky played great defense. Bringing in Gar helped us a lot, and all of a sudden, we were a team, a good team. We felt good going into the playoffs. John was coaching us well. Everything kind of fit together. We had confidence going into the playoffs."

Phoenix's opening playoff opponent in the Western Conference semifinals was Seattle, a team that had some talented players such as Slick Watts, "Downtown" Freddy Brown, and Tom Burleson. The team's head coach was none other than Bill Russell. "I think, down deep, the team knew it was going to be tough, having to go up against Seattle," McCoy said. "But there was some hope because of the nice run to the playoffs."

"We thought we could beat Seattle," said Westphal. "We felt like we had a better team than they did, and that if we played well, we could win."

"I didn't think the Sonics could handle us inside," said Perry. "They had a good home-court advantage, but it didn't matter to us where we played."

"Seattle was always a tough place to win," Colangelo said.

"I thought it would be a very close series, but I thought it would be tough to beat Seattle," added Erickson.

After losing Game 1, 102–99, at the Seattle Center Coliseum on April 13, the Suns rebounded to win Game 2 two nights later, also in the Great Northwest, by a score of 116–111. Three days later at home, the Suns rode strong first and third quarters to a 103–91 victory in Game 3. Two nights later, on April 20 at home again, Phoenix took a commanding 3–1 series lead by defeating the SuperSonics, 130–114. Westphal scored 39 points and had five steals, and Erickson scored 31 points. Five days later, in Game 5 at Seattle, despite 27 points and five steals from Westphal and 24 points from Erickson, the Suns fell, 114–108. Two nights later in Game 6 at home, they pulled away in the second and third quarters en route to a 123–112 triumph for a 4–2 series win.

"Our inside game is what made the difference, and Westphal and Heard had monster series," said Perry.

"Going up there and winning as we did was huge," Colangelo said. "Seattle was a pretty good team, so that was a real confidence builder."

"To be successful in the playoffs," said Wetzel, "two things have to happen—you have to be playing well at that time and you can't have any serious injuries. Well, we started playing better towards the end of the season, and we carried it over into the playoffs. We were playing at a high level."

Phoenix's opponent in the Western Conference finals was Golden State, the defending NBA champions. The Warriors were stocked with great talent in the form of hotshot Rick Barry, Phil Smith, and Jamaal Wilkes. The Suns had played the Warriors six times during the regular season, winning only two. "But we still felt confident going into the series," said Heard. "We felt that we had as good a chance to win the championship as anybody. And the fans … it was crazy. The media called our arena 'The Madhouse on McDowell.' Once we started winning, it was unbelievable. Then, once we got into the playoffs and beat Seattle, every game, the fans got wilder and wilder. They played a huge part in us winning games at home."

"Golden State was favored, and for good reason," Westphal said. "We knew it would be an upset for us to be able to beat them. Our mindset was, 'We're just going to go out there and make them beat us. We're not going to back off.' We weren't under any delusions that we were favored or should be favored."

"It was going to take something special for us to beat Golden State," said Erickson.

"It wasn't like we feared Golden State. We just took them one game at a time," Perry said. "We felt like we could beat the Warriors. We didn't feel we were out of any game simply because of the names on the back of the jerseys of the other team. It's basketball. If you don't do the things right, you get beat. They had some good ballplayers, but we were tough."

After a tight opening quarter of Game 1 on May 2 at the Oakland-Alameda County Coliseum Arena (now Oracle Arena), the Warriors ran away with a 128–103 victory. Even in defeat, Adams had a terrific game with 19 points, 14 rebounds, and six assists.

"We just got crushed," Awtrey said, "but sometimes it's better to be crushed than to lose by two points. You can just throw it away and say, 'Geez, we didn't play very well,' and it's out of your system. Whereas if you lose by one or two, it's 'Man, we played as well as we can, and we didn't beat those guys.'"

The Suns came back three nights later in Game 2, also in Oakland, to tie the series with a 108–101 win. Westphal had 31 points, while Sobers had 23 points, five rebounds, and four assists. Heard had 19 points, 12 rebounds, four steals, and three blocked shots.

"After they blew us out in Game 1, John made some adjustments," said Perry. "One was the substitution pattern for us. Sometimes I'd play a lot, and sometimes Keith would play a lot. Keith was a better scorer than I was, but I was a better rebounder. Defensively, sometimes John switched Gar on Rick Barry, and I guarded Jamaal Wilkes, which kind of threw them off. Phil Smith had scored 51 points in a game against us during the regular season, so we put Ricky on him instead of Westphal. That made a difference. And we bounced back. The fact that we beat them on their home court in the second game, that really had us pumped up."

In Game 3 two nights later on May 7 at Phoenix, the Suns squandered a five-point halftime lead and lost, 99–91. But two days later, also in front of their frenzied fans, they recovered and, behind Erickson's 28 points and six rebounds, won a thriller, 133–129, in double overtime to even the series, 2–2. Heard scored 22 points and pulled down 18 rebounds, while Adams scored 19 points and had 16 boards.

Three nights later in Game 5 at Golden State, the Suns lost, 111–95. Facing a 3–2 series deficit, they returned home, and in Game 6 on May 14, evened the series to force a seventh game by virtue of a heart stopping 105–104 victory.

Game 7 was two days later back in Oakland. Could the Suns pull off a miracle and beat the vaunted Warriors on their home court again to advance to their first-ever NBA Finals? They certainly could. They trailed by only four points after one quarter and by just six points at halftime. They were losing, but they were no doubt sticking around. They outscored the home team by eight points in the third quarter and were in the lead, 67–65, entering the fourth quarter. They outscored the Warriors, 27–21, in the final period for a 94–86 upset that crowned them Western Conference champions.

"Somebody made a late steal and threw the ball to me up ahead for a dunk that put us up by five or six points with only about 40 seconds left," recalled Adams. "We knew then that the Warriors couldn't catch us. There were no threes [three-point shots] back then. We knew we'd won even though the game wasn't over yet, so we started celebrating in our minds. We finally exhaled a little bit and said, 'Wow! We *are* good this year and we *do* have a team.'"

"I remember thinking, 'This is remarkable,'" said Erickson.

"I don't think we talked about the championship round for a couple hours but certainly by the next day," Adams said.

Heard scored 21 points and had 12 rebounds, while Adams put forth an amazing effort with 18 points and 20 rebounds. Westphal added 21 points.

"Keith Erickson was a big contributor in the playoffs, particularly in the Golden State series," said McCoy. "He had some huge offensive games and was a vital part of the Suns moving on to the finals. Unfortunately, he got hurt and his playing time in the championship series was limited."

"We had a good team," said Westphal, "and when we just kept hanging around, we gave ourselves a chance to get an upset in Game 7. Things went our way in that game. We made some plays, and they got a little shaky for whatever reason, and then we made a couple more plays, and it was too late for them to come back. That's kind of the way it is in Game 7. Anybody can win one game, and we did what we had to do to get ourselves to that game."

"It was our defense that won the series for us," Perry said.

"We had a couple home games against Golden State that we should've lost, but the fans would not let us lose," said Heard. "We kept playing the same way we had been. There was a fight between Ricky Sobers and Rick Barry early in Game 7 with punches thrown, and Ricky came out on top. That kind of changed the whole tone of the game. Everything changed after that. We became more aggressive, and Golden State wasn't as aggressive as they normally were. We ended up beating the best team in the league, winning Game 7 at their place."

"Everybody felt that kind of took the starch out of Barry," McCoy said. "He just didn't have the intensity the rest of the way, and the Suns really took it over. They had a lot of energy, a lot of intensity, the entire series actually. Golden State probably thought they were going to have a breeze before the series started, but they got surprised. The Suns were definitely the aggressors in Game 7."

"The Warriors definitely had some dissension. They weren't clicking," Wetzel said. "In the last game, some of their players were giving each other some dirty looks. Something wasn't right with that team, whether it was the Sobers-Barry fight, the pressure, or they sensed that we were coming back on them. They weren't quite as together as we were. We just kept pressing forward and performing, making big shots."

Said Bianchi, "The Warriors weren't hitting on all cylinders."

"We came up big every time we needed to," said Awtrey. "Keith Erickson knocked down some big shots, and Ricky shut down Barry pretty well."

"That series gave us all kinds of confidence that we could play with anybody," Perry said. "I know there's a Cinderella aspect attached to that '76 Suns team, but I don't agree with that. We were a good basketball team that took advantage of the opportunity when it presented itself."

"I think the confidence continued to build, and once you beat a team like Golden State in the conference finals, you gain more confidence," Colangelo said. "To win Game 7 at Golden State was huge. And the reality that we were headed to the finals didn't hit us until the game was just about over."

According to Adams, the true realization that the Suns were a legitimate contender for the NBA title didn't happen until they beat the Warriors in Game 7. "There was talk from the press that we were just pumpkins and that we were just a fairy tale," he recalled. "We all kind of chuckled at that and laughed at it, saying, 'Hey, we're a good team. We don't have the biggest stars in the league, but we're pretty good.' Golden State had gotten better since the previous season when they won it all. That's what we were thinking. It's possible they underestimated us until it was too late. At that point in the season, our confidence was so high. We were thinking, 'Bring on anybody.' We didn't look ahead to a third game, a fifth game … we just knew we had to win four games, and we took it one game at a time, thinking, 'When's the next game? We'll be ready.'"

According to Barry, Golden State should have won the series. "We gave it away," he said. "We had an opportunity to win one of the earlier games at Phoenix. We called a timeout down the stretch. They intentionally fouled one of my teammates, who was going to inbounds the ball. They changed the rule the next year and made it that, in the last two minutes, you could no longer intentionally foul off the basketball. Anyhow, our coaches put somebody else on the free throw line instead of me, and unfortunately, he missed the free throw. Then Phoenix came down the floor, and I believe it was Keith Erickson who hit a huge shot for them. We wound up losing a very close game.

"Then, in Game 7, I had a pretty good first half, but then in the second half I wasn't getting the ball as much. We didn't play the same kind of basketball that we normally played—good team Warriors type of basketball. I probably should've been the guy who said, 'Hey, give me the damn ball,' but when I finally did get it, because I didn't shoot it right away, Al McCoy said I was pouting. I'll never forgive him for that because people pick up on this stuff that people say. If anybody knows me, there's no way in the world that I'm not going to try to win. I tried to do what I thought was best for us to win that game. I remember that game like it was freaking yesterday. It was a very heartbreaking loss. We could've been one of the few teams to ever repeat as champion, and we should've. We should've won the series, there's no question about it, but hey, give Phoenix credit. I'm not taking anything away from them. They did what they had to do under the situation that existed, so more credit to them."

"After the Game 7 win, we had some time before our flight. You didn't charter in those days," said Awtrey. "We went out to eat at a local place and had a good time. It was a real fun plane ride home. We were feeling pretty good about ourselves. We got back to Phoenix, and we weren't paying attention to things. We weren't thinking anything big. And, as the plane got to the gate, the pilot announced, 'Will the Suns players please get off last?' So the other passengers got off the plane, and then we got off the plane and walked into the airport, and the whole place was just rockin'. People were everywhere! It was reasonably late at night, so we were shocked at how many people came out there. I was thinking, 'This is a big deal, isn't it?' There were 5,000 people there *in the airport*. People were sitting on exhibit boxes in the terminal, and others were sitting on a car or two that were advertising something. We felt like rock stars! That was the first time I'd ever seen anything like that in anything I'd been associated with."

"We barely *needed* a plane to get back to Phoenix," Westphal laughed. "We were really feeling good. And then to have half of Phoenix, it seemed like, waiting at the airport, that was quite a shot of adrenaline for us."

Two nights later, the Boston Celtics finished off the Cleveland Cavaliers in six games to win the Eastern Conference title. The NBA Finals would be the Suns versus the Celtics.

"Boston had some really talented players, but we were going to give it all we had," said Erickson.

"We felt like we could knock off the Celtics, there's no doubt about it," Awtrey said. "We knew it would be a heck of a series, but we felt really good about it. We were a talented team, we matched up well against them, and we were ready to go."

5

THE '75-'76 CELTICS

The 1975–76 Boston Celtics wanted to forget about their defeat to Washington in the previous season's Eastern Conference title series and bring home a second NBA championship in three years. One newcomer who they hoped would help achieve that goal was All-Star guard Charlie Scott, whom they traded for from Phoenix in exchange for Paul Westphal. During the 1974–75 season, Scott, who Boston drafted a few years back but had already elected to play in the ABA, averaged 24.8 points per game for the Suns. "Red Auerbach had difficulty with Westphal's agent," said Tom Heinsohn. "He decided he was going to trade him because he couldn't sign him. Scott took Don Chaney's place after Chaney jumped to St. Louis of the American Basketball Association. Charlie became very important to our team."

"When that trade went down, a lot of eyebrows were arched on both sides," said Bob Ryan. "One was that Phoenix would think that highly of Westphal, and two, oh boy, this will be interesting, Charlie and Jo Jo [White] … are they going to be able to coexist? They're both high-powered offensive players who have the ball a lot. How's this all going to work out? Well, I remember noticing right away at training camp that they were hanging out, bonding, and trying to make it work. It was never an issue."

It really should not have come as a surprise, though. "I was ecstatic going to a team with the legacy of the Celtics," said Scott. "And Jo Jo and I had been best friends since we were both on the Olympic team in 1968. Not only was he my best friend, he was also my backcourt mate. He was a fantastic basketball player. I thought we were just as good as any backcourt in the history of the game."

"Charlie became our starting two-guard after playing point guard for Phoenix," said Heinsohn. "He was a scorer, but Jo Jo ran the team. When we got Charlie, we talked to him. I said, 'Charlie, they made you the scapegoat wherever you went. If you didn't score 40 points, they'd be all over your case. You won't have to score 40 points here, but we expect you to play defense because we believe you're a terrific defensive player.' And he just jumped right in and did what we asked him to do. He scored, but defensively he really helped us be aggressive."

"Charlie was a slight kind of guy, very thin, but very athletic," Rick Barry said. "He could get to the basket and shoot the jumper. He was an outstanding offensive player."

Three other newcomers to the Celtics in 1975–76 who Heinsohn hoped would be bench help were power forward Tom Boswell, guard Jerome Anderson, and small forward Ed Searcy. Boswell was a first-round draft pick out of the University of South Carolina. Anderson was a third-round draft choice from West Virginia University, while Searcy was signed as a free agent.

"Tom Boswell could've been a great basketball player, but he wasn't focused on playing, and he subsequently got in a lot of trouble through the years," said Heinsohn.

"'Boz' was raw at that time as far as talent, and I don't think he really applied himself," said Steve Kuberski, who was back in Beantown after spending a short time with Milwaukee and Buffalo.

"Jerome could really guard people and could make shots," Kevin Stacom said. "Ed was very athletic and a very explosive guy. He could rebound the ball and could score inside."

Searcy, who spent a very short time with the team early in the season, was in awe of many of his teammates. He was 22 years old and said that he grew up watching everybody on the team. He said that, after he started playing with them, they were really good guys. Naturally, they put him through the whole rookie thing like having to go get the hotel keys, pick up the luggage at the airport, little things like that. But he didn't mind. He said that he came in and busted ass and beat out eight other players to make the team. He started an early exhibition game against the Knicks at Madison Square Garden. He said tongue-in-cheek that it was his bad luck that nobody got hurt that year, that nobody had a sprained ankle, nobody caught a cold. He said that it was like a paradoxical feeling—if the team lost, then he could have played. If the team won, then he would not have played.

John Havlicek actually dealt with a foot injury for most of the season, but that was about it. "He did the best he could, which was pretty good," said Heinsohn.

"We had a starting frontcourt of Dave, Paul, and John, with Don Nelson coming off the bench, and we had Jo Jo and Charlie as the starting guards," said Stacom. "That's a high talent level."

"Paul and Dave were the backbone of that team," added Scott. "Their rebounding and defense were the keys to our success."

"They were aggressive," said former New York Knick Walt Frazier in an interview on Classic Sports Network (now ESPN Classic). "Cowens provided the impetus. He was an adrenaline-type player. Paul Silas, relentless on the glass as well. So it bordered on being dirty, but I think they were just a very aggressive team."

"We practiced hard, and we respected what each player brought to the court. Every guy knew his responsibility," said Scott. "We never worried about the other team. We thought we were good enough to beat anybody. We were a hell of a team."

"I hated [the Celtics]. I hated them," said Frazier. "I hated anything green other than money. As a kid growing up, say when I was in college, the Celtics always won, so I rooted for the underdog, so I hated them, but I admired and respected them."

The 1975–76 Celtics were a very consistent team. After a 5–5 start, they won 14 of their next 16 games and stood at 19–7 following a 111–97 win at Philadelphia on December 20. They reeled off seven straight wins in late January and early February to stand at 35–13 on February 7. They cruised the rest of the way to a 54–28 final record and first place in the Atlantic Division, eight games ahead of the 76ers and Braves.

Cowens averaged 19 points, 16 rebounds, and 4.2 assists per game. White averaged 18.9 points and 5.4 assists per contest. "Dave was probably one of the greatest undersized centers in the game," said Barry. "He was aggressive, mobile, a tough defender, could shoot the mid-range shot, go to the basket ... a heck of a competitor."

"He was a lot more athletic than people realize," said Stacom. "He was very explosive and very fast. He played the center position almost like a linebacker, setting picks and going through picks. He was just a great player."

"Dave has got to be the quickest big man I've ever seen," Jim Ard said. "And for a big man, that's just a strength you don't see. He was hard-nosed and would risk his body to go after a ball."

Said Glenn McDonald, "He was just ferocious. He was one of the hardest workers on the team and backed down to no one. Most opponents did not like playing against him because of how physical he was."

"During the '75–'76 season, Jo Jo was at the utter peak of his career," said Bob Ryan. "He was a great offensive player. He was a combo, too, in that he could play point guard or shooting guard. He was just a pro. He was one of the great guards in the league at that point. It was a prime time for Jo Jo."

According to Searcy, White had a halftime ritual that amazed him. He said that he was the only player he ever saw do this. He said that, at halftime of every game, he would come in the locker room and smoke a cigarette, one cigarette! Searcy was shocked but added that White was a fantastic player.

Scott averaged 17.6 points per game, while Havlicek hung up 17 points per contest. "Charlie was a high-energy individual who could score in bunches," said McDonald. "He was very, very competitive, too."

"Charlie was very durable," Stacom said. "He was a great player, very talented. He was quick and could create his own shot."

"I don't even know where to begin with John Havlicek," said Ryan. "When I came along in '69 and for the next five years, in my opinion, he was a better player than either Jerry West or Oscar Robertson. He was the best all-around player in the league on both ends of the floor. He was doing triple-doubles routinely before we had a word for it."

"John was the ultimate pro," Kuberski said. "He performed every night, and he was meticulous in how he performed and how he prepared for every game. You talk about a coach on the floor, he definitely was that. He was the glue of our team."

Searcy said that, in practice, he had to *cover* Havlicek. He said that he would run through all the screens of Silas and Cowens and that, one day after practice, he asked him why he never got tired. He said that Havlicek told him a phenomenal story. When Havlicek was in Martins Ferry, Ohio, his high school was about 10 miles from his house. He lived on a farm. He would jog to school in the morning, and he would jog back home after practice. That's 20 miles a day, 120 miles a week, 480 miles a month, more than 4,000 miles a year. And he never smoked or drank. So Searcy came to realize why Havlicek never got tired.

"Havlicek was like a robot, the bionic man," Heinsohn said in an NBA TV video. "People at Harvard were doing studies on his heart rate because he had this stamina, never stopped running.

Added Scott, "John probably was the greatest small forward who ever played as far as endurance."

"John was a very unusual person and player. He was great in both categories," Stacom said. "He was great for me as a young player, very supportive, always willing to help out. He was a natural leader by example."

Also in 1975–76, Silas averaged 10.7 points and 12.7 rebounds per game.

"Paul was a strong individual, strong willed, strong on the boards, and had great perseverance," said McDonald. "He wasn't the greatest scorer, but that wasn't his job. He was a rebounder and a defensive player."

"Paul just worked his heart out to play the game," Ard said.

When called upon, the Celtics' reserve players did exactly what they were asked to do. "Don Nelson was the ultimate cerebral forward, a player of his times," said Ryan. "He knew how to play, knew all the tricks, *and* was a great shooter. He led the league in field-goal percentage in 1974–75 at age 34, going on 35, and 90 percent were foul-line jump shots. The other 10 percent were off of offensive rebounds. He had a great up-fake. He was just a marvel at knowing how to play the game."

"Don was one of those guys who you called the scholar," McDonald said. "He wasn't that athletic, but he knew how to place himself in position to get the job done. He was always a hard worker and very, very smooth in what he did. He was a very solid player."

"'Nellie' was our sixth man," said Scott. "He was very efficient at what he did. He knew what his responsibilities were, and he took care of business."

"Glenn McDonald fit in perfectly for the type of role that a backup to Havlicek would have," said Ryan. "He'd run the wing, and he was very fast. He played in a lot of games and had a role."

"Steve Kuberski was a very solid player who could shoot the ball," McDonald said. "If we wanted to pull a post player from the block, Steve could always step out from the outside and still shoot the jumper. He was kind of like a stretch four is now. He was a very hard-working individual and definitely a team player."

"Steve was a tough guy, a very good rebounder, and could score the ball also," said Stacom. "He knew his role, and he did it very well."

"Kevin Stacom was all energy, a very good playmaking guard, someone who never gave up," McDonald said. "He dove for loose balls, was just a hard-working individual."

"When Kevin got a chance, I thought he performed well," Kuberski said. "Jim Ard was a good backup center and provided what you want out of a backup center."

"Jim was very athletic and strong. He rebounded the ball well," said Stacom. "Tom Boswell was a very skilled big man. He could rebound and do a lot of different things. Every time he got a chance to play, he did very well."

As for Boston's head coach, most of the players adored Heinsohn. "I loved everything about Tommy," said Scott. "He allowed the ballplayers to be themselves. He didn't put any responsibilities on you that he thought you shouldn't do. All he wanted you to do was be respectful to what you were supposed to do and be prepared to play when the time called for it."

"Tom was a high-energy individual," McDonald said. "He was very knowledgeable of the game. He tried to use his players the best he could in whatever situation he needed. You never knew what he was going to do because he didn't have a set plan all the time, but he understood the game and could adjust to what other coaches were doing."

Added Stacom, "Tom was very good at maintaining the traditional Celtics style of play, really emphasized pushing the ball up the court."

The players were also big fans of assistant coach John Killilea. "John was an excellent defensive coach," said Stacom. "He really broke things down very simply during game preparation and while the game was going on."

"John had a brilliant offensive mind, too," Ryan said. "He was one of the legendary all-time high school coaches in the state of Massachusetts. When I came in in 1969–70, there were no assistant coaches in the league at all. He was one of the very early assistants. He was truly a right-hand man. He was very valuable."

During the second half of the 1975–76 season, the Celtics were having trouble winning on the road. "They went into the playoffs with a strong element of doubt," said Ryan.

"I didn't know if we were strong enough to get through the East, let alone win the whole thing," said Kuberski. "I thought Washington, with Elvin Hayes and Wes Unseld, was probably the strongest team in the East."

Boston's first playoff opponent in the Eastern Conference semifinals was the Buffalo Braves, who had superstar Bob McAdoo plus other talented players such as Randy Smith, Jim McMillian, and John Shumate, the latter who had been traded from the Suns to the Braves in the Gar Heard deal earlier in the season. "Buffalo was a tough, excellent team," said Stacom.

"I thought we had more talent than Buffalo, though," said Ard. "If we stayed out of foul trouble, I thought we'd be just fine. I figured that it would probably go five or six games."

Ard was correct. Boston ousted the Braves, four games to two. The Celtics won Game 1, 107–98, on April 21 at the Boston Garden. Cowens had a monster game with 30 points, 17 rebounds, and seven assists. White scored 27 points, while Havlicek put up 22 points but injured his left foot and would miss the next three games. Two nights later, again at home, the Celtics defeated Buffalo, 101–96. Cowens again came up big with 27 points and 18 rebounds. Nelson had a nice game with 22 points and six rebounds. Two days later, in Game 3 at the Buffalo Memorial Auditorium, things looked good for Boston as they had a 24–12 lead after one quarter. The Braves recovered, though, and took a one-point halftime lead en route to a 98–93 victory. Three nights later, in Game 4 on April 28, again at home, Buffalo evened the series at two games apiece with a 124–122 triumph. Cowens was all-world with a near triple-double—29 points, 26 rebounds, and eight assists. White scored 28 points and had 11 assists, and Nelson hung up 27 points.

Two nights later, in Game 5 back at the Boston Garden, the Celtics won, 99–88, behind 30 points and 16 rebounds from Cowens. Silas was huge, too, with 15 points and 22 rebounds. Two days later, in Game 6 at Buffalo, the Celtics defeated the Braves, 104–100, in the series clincher. Scott scored 31 points and had eight assists, and White scored 23 points.

"The Celtics managed to win the series, but it was a struggle," said Ryan.

Boston's opponent in the Eastern Conference finals was the Cleveland Cavaliers, who won the Central Division with a 49–33 record and beat Washington in a thrilling conference semifinal series, four games to three. There were many observers who felt the Cavs did the Celtics a favor by ousting the Bullets. "We didn't have the size to match up with Washington, the team we lost to in the playoffs the year before. So that was a break there," Kuberski said.

"The Celtics got lucky because Jim Chones, Cleveland's starting center, broke his ankle in a freak accident two days before the start of the series," said Ryan. "It put all the pressure in the middle on aging Nate Thurmond."

"Cleveland had some pretty good players, though, like Bingo Smith and Jim Cleamons," said Kuberski. "But we were pretty confident that we could beat them."

In Game 1 on May 6 in Boston, the Celtics took a 32–20 lead after one quarter, but the Cavaliers fought back to tie the score at 77 entering the fourth quarter. The Celtics, though, wound up winning, 111–99. Havlicek scored 26 points, Silas had 21 points and 11 rebounds, and White added 20 points. Three days later, in Game 2, again in Boston, the Cavs raced to a pair of nine-point leads and had a 73–70 advantage early in the fourth quarter. But Havlicek, Cowens, and Scott combined for 11 straight points to put Boston up, 81–73. Cleveland cut it to 83–81, but the Celtics stretched their lead to 89–81 en route to a 94–89 victory. White scored 24 points and Havlicek had 20. Silas grabbed 19 rebounds.

The series moved to the Coliseum in Richfield, Ohio, for Game 3 on May 11. The Celtics trailed, 43–38, at halftime, at which point Thurmond had held Cowens to just eight points. The Cavaliers kept the lead until the visitors tied the score at 62 with 9:56 left in the game. The Cavs scored six straight points to go up 68–62 on the way to an 83–78 triumph. White scored 22 points, Cowens was a monster with 19 points and 20 rebounds, while Silas had 12 points and 21 rebounds. Three nights later, again at the Coliseum, the Celtics went from trailing, 79–77, with eight minutes remaining in the game to trailing, 97–83, with 2:20 left. They wound up losing, 106–87, tying the series at two games apiece.

Recurring effects from his earlier foot injury kept Havlicek out of Boston's starting lineup in Game 5 at the Boston Garden on May 16. He would see action only if it became critical. And critical it would become for the Celtics. The game was another frantic battle, with the Cavs up, 23–22, after one quarter and the score tied, 42–42, at the half. Thurmond, who was doing a masterful job on Cowens, picked up his fifth foul early in the third quarter. He played with caution until fouling out with 5:03 left in the game. Soon after, Red Auerbach raced to the bench when Heinsohn was ejected and immediately inserted Havlicek into the game. "Hondo" failed to score from the field, but he was the inspirational lift his team needed. He did sink two free throws with 11 seconds to go to send the Celtics to a 99–94 victory and a 3–2 series lead. Cowens scored 26 points and had 11 rebounds and six assists. Silas totaled 13 rebounds.

Two nights later, in Game 6 at the Coliseum, the game was once again tight from start to finish. Boston was up, 22–19, after one quarter. The Cavaliers led, 46–43, at halftime. They reeled off eight straight points to forge ahead, 69–61, late in the third quarter. The Celtics pulled to within 69–67 after three. The game was tied at 69, then at 76, and again at 78. A three-point play by Thurmond gave the Cavs an 81–78 advantage. A Cowens tip-in put Boston up, 82–81. The Cavaliers went up, 83–82, then White hit a long bomb to give Boston an 84–83 lead with three minutes left. Cleveland got the lead back at 85–84. The Cavs stole the ball from Cowens but couldn't turn it into points. White hit another from downtown for an 86–85 Celtics lead. Scott then stole the ball and drove for a layup. The Celtics went on to a 94–87 victory, winning the series in six games. White scored 29 points, while Cowens had 21 points and 18 rebounds.

"Had Chones not gotten hurt, Cleveland very possibly could've won the series. We'll never know what would've happened had Chones not gotten hurt," said Ryan. "Thurmond played great, he really played great. He matched Cowens very well. He always played great against Cowens.

Those two had an unknown, great rivalry. They didn't play enough games against one another for people to realize how good it was. Even without Chones, the Cavaliers held their own. The Celtics won a very tough Game 5 and then went out to Cleveland for Game 6, and Charlie Scott [20 points] came up big."

Boston was on its way to face the Phoenix Suns in the NBA Finals.

"For some reason, we didn't match up real well with Golden State, so we got another break by Phoenix beating them," said Kuberski. "It also gave us the home-court advantage in the finals, something we wouldn't have had against the Warriors."

"Phoenix caught Golden State napping a little bit," Stacom said. "We were capable of beating Golden State, but we had a better chance against Phoenix. I thought we had a good chance of beating them, but you couldn't nap on them. They had tough matchups themselves. Paul Westphal had become a star by then. He was a real tough cover. He was very deceptive. He had a great crossover move. He was pretty much ambidextrous. Ricky Sobers was a tough guy. Alvan Adams was real quick, very athletic, very talented."

"Phoenix was a similar type team to us," said Heinsohn. "Adams was almost a duplicate of Cowens without the ferocity. He could pass and shoot the ball outside. So it was like playing ourselves at times. They played up-tempo basketball. They had some really good players."

"But we were still confident that we could beat Phoenix," said Kuberski.

6

SPLITSVILLE

Boston swept the regular-season season series from Phoenix in 1975–76, four games to none. The Celtics defeated the Suns, 112–106, on December 26 in Phoenix. They beat them, 114–100 on January 21 at Boston. Three weeks later, on February 13 in Phoenix, the Celtics won again, 109–108. They routed the Suns, 122–102, on March 31 at Boston. The Celtics had actually won six straight games against the Suns dating back to the 1974–75 season.

"Boston had its way with us that '75–'76 season," said Curtis Perry. "It wasn't a matter of having to get accustomed to how they'd play. We knew how they'd play."

"They were just way more physical than us," Alvan Adams said.

The first two games of the finals would be played in Boston. "I knew, from my playing days, that the Boston Garden was a tough place to play," said Al Bianchi. "We could never beat them there. Every time we went up there, we had a police escort. And I knew that, when you go up to Boston, you can't just be good, you've got to be 10 points better because you're not going to get the breaks."

"It was fun being around Al when we were playing the Celtics because he'd been beaten by them so many times as a player, he had a real built-in hatred for them," said Paul Westphal. "He always had stories for us about why we should go get the hated Celtics."

As for Westphal going up against his former team, he had no vendettas. "I didn't really have any fear because I was used to those guys," he said.

"I also knew how good they were. It was just something that was really exciting to do."

"We went into the series with our eyes wide open," said Jerry Colangelo. "We were a young team—think about it—with two rookies in the starting lineup playing for the championship, playing on one of the toughest courts ever, the old Boston Garden, against an excellent Celtics team. The whole idea in the playoffs is that you have to win your home games, and you have to steal one on the road if you don't have the home-court advantage."

"We all felt, though, that we had a legitimate shot of beating Boston," said Adams. "I knew we had an ace in the hole in Paul because he taught us, 'Watch out for Havlicek. If you back him down, sometimes he'll just grab your shorts and pull you down on top of him.' Paul knew all those little tricks and tendencies Boston did from playing with them before. He was a big part of our preparation for that. I knew when I was playing against Dave Cowens, I was going to have plenty of bruises and I was going to have whiplash. He was a great center who was quick enough to guard the quick centers like myself and Bob McAdoo, but he could also pound the big guys like Bob Lanier and Nate Thurmond. He was that rare combination of strength and speed that you didn't see very often."

According to Ed Searcy, Adams would shoot jump shots. He said that he was like a modern-day center—he didn't play in the hole. He said that brought Cowens outside, which opened up the center for his teammates to drive.

"There was a lot of commonality in our games," Cowens said of Adams in the 2001 *Boston Globe* story.

In Game 1 on May 23, the Celtics won, 98–87, behind 25 points, 21 rebounds, and 10 assists from Cowens. White scored 22 points, while Havlicek came off the bench to score 16. Adams led all scorers with 26 points and had eight rebounds.

After trailing, 25–24, after one quarter of Game 2 four nights later, the Celtics forged ahead, 46–41, at halftime and then blistered Phoenix, 34–16, in the third quarter for an 80–57 lead en route to a 105–90 victory. Havlicek came off the bench again to score 23 points. Cowens scored 16 points and had 12 rebounds. Westphal scored 28 points, while Adams had 19 points and 15 rebounds in a losing cause.

"We controlled those first two games," said Steve Kuberski. "I think we pretty much led most of the way."

"We didn't adjust well," said Perry. "There was a lot of very, very physical play."

"I think Boston was just better in those first two games. They played well, and we didn't," Bianchi said.

"They pounded us and did what they wanted to do," said Adams. "I think we thought we were just beat up and that we needed to respond and play tougher, be more physical, make our cuts, knock guys' arms off of us, take the ball to the hole and make the referee see the fouls, and not be complacent and be the aggressor."

"Charlie had an axe to grind with Phoenix, and he played great," said Tom Heinsohn. "And Jo Jo just carried the team."

Recalled Al McCoy, "The Boston media, the newspapers, radio, and TV people were saying, 'Who are these guys from the desert? They don't belong in the same arena as the Celtics.'"

Games 3 and 4 would be played in Phoenix. "You go on the road in the playoffs, and if you're playing a good team, you shoot for a split," John Wetzel said. "Well, we didn't get it, but we felt really, really comfortable at home, even playing the Celtics. We weren't intimidated."

"A lot of times, that's what happens," Awtrey added. "Everybody says, 'Oh-h-h-h, you just lost two games,' and they think you're out of it. We weren't down in the dumps when we were down 0–2 because we were going home. You go home and hold serve there. We felt good about it."

"We'd all been around enough, except Ricky and Alvan, that we all knew the old cliché that, until somebody wins a road game, the series hasn't started," said Westphal. "We believed that we'd go home and win one and win another to even up the series. We knew we had to win in the Boston Garden sometime, so you crossed the first two off, but we still felt that we could play with those guys and very possibly beat them. So we didn't feel dead after losing those two in Boston."

"Everybody wrote us off," said Heard. "But we knew, going back home, that our fans would be behind us and we had a chance to win those two games. We never thought that we were going to lose the series. We never did."

"Our job was to go home and win the next two, and we start over again," Colangelo said. "The home court is always an advantage. I always maintain that the enthusiasm of your fans can only help you and could be the difference maker with the pressure as great as it is in these games during the playoffs."

Suns fans were lined up outside, sleeping overnight in attempting to purchase tickets for Games 3 and 4. "Those fans were just as great as the fans in Boston," said McCoy. "Jerry Colangelo was handing out coffee and donuts. It really brought the NBA to life in Phoenix. It was an exciting time and an exciting team. They were young, and these guys didn't know that they shouldn't win."

On the other side of the ledger, the Celtics were feeling pretty good about themselves and their 2–0 lead in the series. "We were pretty confident," Kuberski said.

In Game 3 on May 30, the Suns, behind the raucous Phoenix fans, jumped out to a nine-point lead after the first quarter and upped that lead to 52–39 at halftime. A late Celtics run fell short as the home team hung on for a 105–98 victory. Adams had a monster game with 33 points and 14 rebounds. White led the Celtics with 24 points, while Cowens had 13 points and 17 rebounds.

In Game 4 three nights later, Phoenix had a 35–30 lead after one quarter, a 60–57 lead at the half, and an 87–80 advantage after three quarters before hanging on for a 109–107 triumph. Westphal scored 28 points and had nine assists and five rebounds, while Heard had 19 points and 15 boards. Adams scored 20 points and Sobers added 14.

"Ricky Sobers was a pretty cocky kid. He was aggravating, but he was a pretty good player," said Kuberski.

For Boston, White scored 25 points and dished out five assists, Cowens had 22 points and 12 rebounds, and Silas had 18 points and 14 rebounds.

"In Games 3 and 4, we got big games from the people we needed them from," Bianchi said.

"In the first two games," said Ryan, "John MacLeod and Colangelo were bitching about the referees, but the refs really turned it around in Game 3. There's no question that there was a whole different outlook, a different approach. The Celtics felt very unfairly treated by the officials in Games 3 and 4."

Whatever the case may have been regarding the officiating, one thing was certain—the series was now deadlocked at two games apiece, with the all-important Game 5 set for two nights later on June 4 back in Boston.

7

BLOWOUT

Many of the Boston fans in attendance at Game 5 of the 1976 Finals could have been inducted into the Inebriation Hall of Fame, for the contest was on a Friday night and didn't start until after 9 p.m. So there were four to five hours of drinking time for fans from the time their workweeks ended to the start of the game.

On top of that, the fans were none too happy about the officiating in games 3 and 4 and negative comments about the Celtics made by Rick Barry, who was working with Brent Musburger on the CBS telecast. "You don't do that, and so Boston Garden was now in full venom with Rick Barry and with the referees," said sportscaster Al Trautwig on Classic Sports Network.

"We had a lot of drunks behind the bench," said Al Bianchi. "They were getting a little rowdy. I had to keep some of our players from going in after them."

Moreover, the Boston Garden was ... well ... the Boston Garden. Said Walt Frazier on the same program on Classic Sports Network, "First of all, the Garden was the most intimidating arena in the league—the parquet floor, the hallowed walls, the rafters adorned with all their championship banners—so you're already intimidated going in there. Now a very hostile crowd like that, so you wouldn't give the Suns much of an opportunity to win that game. The dead spots [on the floor] were the main thing about it. I remember once I went behind my back [in his playing days], and I *still* don't know where the ball is."

To make matters worse for the Suns, they had lost 12 straight games in Boston dating all the way back to the 1971–72 season. And the Celtics raced to a 13–3 lead, the last points of which came on a jumper by John Havlicek, back in the starting lineup. John MacLeod called his second timeout.

"When the Suns got down early in that first quarter," said Al McCoy, "you thought, 'Uh oh, I don't know what's going to happen.'"

Things only got worse for Phoenix.

Gar Heard stepped out of bounds to give the ball back to Boston, and Paul Silas hit a straightaway jumper from behind the free throw line to make it 15–3. After Alvan Adams swished a jumper from the left side, Havlicek swished one from the right side. Then, after a turnover by Ricky Sobers, Havlicek laid one in off a long pass from Silas, was fouled by Adams, and converted the free throw to make the score 20–5. With the score 24–10, Sobers and Heard both missed shots, and the ball was volleyballed to Jo Jo White, who dribbled up the court and, on the right baseline, flipped a behind-the-back pass to Havlicek, who swished a long rainbow jumper from the right baseline with a defender in his face. That made the score 26–10. After a missed jumper by Dick Van Arsdale, Dave Cowens nailed a jumper from behind the free throw line to increase the Boston lead to 18 points. Timeout, Suns.

"Very unusual to see a coach call three timeouts in the first period," commented Mendy Rudolph on CBS's telecast.

White hit a wide-open bank shot that made the score 34–14. "I remember how fast the Celtics came out," recalled Sobers in the 2001 *Boston Globe* story. "Before we could even blink, we were down 20."

"Boston was killing us," MacLeod said in the same article. "I said, 'Are they ever going to slow down?'"

"We were really reeling," said MacLeod in the video *Great Moments in the NBA: Awesome Endings.*

After Jim Ard hit a wide-open jumper from the right baseline as the first quarter ended, the Celtics were in command, 36–18.

Sobers opened the second-quarter scoring by swishing a jump shot from the right baseline. The home team came right back, however. White drove for an open layup. After a missed jumper by Paul Westphal, Steve

Kuberski rebounded a missed shot by Ard and banked it in for a 40–20 Boston advantage.

"We couldn't stop them from running, so I decided to try Phil Lumpkin," MacLeod told the *Globe*. "He was a pounder, a guy who dribbled a lot. I hoped he could slow the game down."

In the same article, Lumpkin said, "We had to just slow it down to a half-court game, run our sets, and get people the touches where they can be effective with the ball."

Plan failed.

Cowens laid in a bank shot off a double-pump pass from Charlie Scott to up the Celtics' lead to 42–20.

At this point, had anyone even hinted that this basketball game would turn out to be "The Greatest Game Ever Played," they would have been sent to a psychiatrist. Boston was simply dominating, and outclassing, the young Suns.

The visitors finally showed some life when Dennis Awtrey hit a jumper, Curtis Perry laid one in, Heard hit one of his patented high, arching jumpers, and Westphal laid one in to pull within 42–28. After Cowens hit one of two free throws, Westphal made a reverse layup off a pretty pass from Adams, and then Adams swished a jumper from the left side to make the score 43–32 with 6:57 remaining in the first half. A few minutes later, the Suns pulled to within 46–39 when, after a turnover by Silas, Heard went in for an easy dunk. The Celtics then went on an 8–2 run, though, that was capped by two Havlicek free throws. Boston was now up by 13 points at 54–41. By halftime, the Celtics expanded their lead to 61–45.

"The first 15 or so minutes of the game was, without question, the best basketball the Celtics played in the entire playoffs. Period," said Bob Ryan. "It looked like it was going to be a knockout blow, particularly because it was at home."

Said Bianchi, "We just didn't play well in that first half."

8

BACK IN IT

"People always ask me," said Alvan Adams, 'What did the coach say to you at halftime?' We were so tuned in, as were the Celtics. I think it's mostly up to the players at that time. But we had eight months of preparation behind us by great coaches who had us prepared. And, as they always say in the playoffs, 'We know the opponents' every play, we know which way Havlicek likes to go, and that Cowens is going to charge in and dive and all of that.' We didn't put a new play in at halftime, we didn't change a lot of stuff.' I don't remember any major personnel changes. It was just, 'Hey, we have to respond. We're two to two. We're the Suns. We're in the finals. Let's respond.'"

"We rarely felt that we were out of a game," said Gar Heard. "That was the mentality of our team during the second half of the season. We played so bad the first half in Game 5, and they played great. So we just said, 'We have to go out and play our game, just get control of the game, control the tempo, and just chip away at their lead.'"

And that is exactly what Phoenix did. The Suns knew they could not afford to allow Boston to come out fast in the third quarter and go up by 20 points. They immediately cut the Celtics' lead to 61–50 on a three-point play by Curtis Perry and a layup by Ricky Sobers. When Jo Jo White hit a technical free throw about halfway through the third quarter to give Boston a 68–57 lead, it was the last time the Celtics would enjoy a double-digit advantage. A three-point play by Sobers with 5:19 left in the quarter cut the Boston lead to 68–64. An uncontested dunk by Sobers made it a two-point game, and then following a Boston timeout, Adams made two free throws to tie the score, 68–68, with less than four minutes to go in the third. It was the first time all night that the Celtics did not have the lead.

From that point on, it was anyone's game.

"It was crazy how they came back," said Steve Kuberski.

According to Ed Searcy, at halftime White said, "These motherfuckers are gonna come back." Searcy said that he was thinking that the Celtics were up by 16 points but that, sure enough, the Suns *did* come back.

"Phoenix never went away," Bob Ryan said.

"I think we just firmed up," said Dennis Awtrey. "It's tough to keep a big lead sometimes. You're up 20, you're shooting the heck out of the ball, everything is going good for you, but then you get a little overconfident, and the losing team starts chipping away. You can come back on that sort of thing."

Said John Wetzel, "I think the nature of our team, with Dick [Van Arsdale], Paul [Westphal], and Alvan and those guys, there was a mindset that they just kept playing. There was no panic, there was no giving in or giving up. They just kept playing, and we just kept plugging away and making shots. We figured it's a long game, and with all the stoppages in play—the timeouts and the free throws—we had a lot of time to get back in the game."

"I probably didn't think the Suns could come back and make a game of it," Al McCoy added. "They surprised everybody. The attitude on this ballclub starting late in the season was that they were always in the game. And, ultimately, they maintained that attitude that they were never going to be out of a game. And they were able to get it turned around."

"At halftime, we made defensive adjustments," said Perry. "We got Boston to slow it down, and we ran. We controlled the boards better in the second half, and we started making shots. You can't just discount that we shot so poorly that first half. When the shots are falling and you're playing defense and rebounding … we stayed in the game. We never, not once, felt like we were going to lose that game."

"I think we came back because we had heart," said Adams.

Now that the Suns had recovered to even the score, they needed to maintain their edge and carry that momentum forward. But Boston broke the deadlock and took a 70–68 lead when Kuberski sank a jumper from the left baseline. A few moments later, Cowens hit a half-hook shot to make the score 72–68. By the end of the third quarter, the Celtics led, 77–72.

To start the fourth quarter, Cowens hit a short turnaround jumper over Awtrey to expand the Boston lead to seven. Nate Hawthorne rebounded a Westphal miss and scored to make it 79–74. A pair of free throws by Cowens and a layup by Charlie Scott pushed the lead to 83–74 with 9:13 remaining. The Suns pulled to within five points, but, a few moments later, a jumper by White with a hand in his face gave the Celtics an 86–79 lead. Perry rebounded his own miss and banked it in to make it 86–81. White hit a wide-open jumper from the left, then Cowens swished a hook shot from the lane to make it 90–81. Adams sank a wide-open jumper from the left baseline to make the score 90–83, and then Havlicek hit a jumper from the right baseline for a 92–83 Boston advantage.

Westphal swished a turnaround rainbow jumper from the right baseline and then hit an open jumper from the right to pull Phoenix within 92–87 with 2:58 remaining. After a Celtics timeout and three possession changes, the Suns cut their deficit to 92–89 with 1:54 to go when Sobers swished an open jumper from the lane. A Silas tip-in off a miss by White gave Boston a 94–89 lead with 1:03 left. The Suns cut it to 94–91 with 52 seconds to go on a turnaround bank shot from the right by Westphal. While Scott brought the ball up the court, Westphal reached in and poked it away to Adams, who fired it back up the court to Westphal. He drove for a layup and was fouled by Scott. He connected on the free throw to tie the score, 94–94, with 39 seconds left. Perhaps even more important was the fact that Scott had fouled out of the game.

Following a Boston timeout, Don Nelson inbounded from half-court and, a few passes later, Scott missed from way beyond the top of the key. Cowens's put-back attempt missed, and he fouled Perry by pushing off as he went for the rebound. With the Celtics over the foul limit, Perry got two free throws. He made the first but missed badly on the second as the ball clanged off the front of the rim. Phoenix had its very first lead of the game at 95–94 with 22 seconds remaining. With Van Arsdale guarding him, Havlicek missed a turnaround jumper from the right baseline, but was fouled by Adams, who reached in. In the process, he fouled out. Hondo made the first free throw but missed the second one. The score was 95–95 with 19 seconds to go. Havlicek's missed free throw was batted by the Suns back out to himself, who passed to White, who passed the ball right back to Havlicek. He dribbled to the right, then threw the ball in to Cowens, who passed it back out to Havlicek, who missed a jumper from the right with Westphal in his face. The rebound went to Westphal with three seconds to go. Westphal called timeout. The Suns argued that he had called time with four seconds left. Actually, he had called time with five seconds left, but it was to no avail. The officials left the three ticks on the clock. With Jim Ard guarding him, Heard inbounded the ball, but Cowens intercepted it. Silas called timeout with one second left before the clock ran out.

There was a problem, though. The Celtics had no timeouts left. The rule stated that, if a team called a timeout even though it had none remaining, it was a technical foul, and the other team received a free throw. Referee Richie Powers was directly facing Silas when he called the timeout, but Powers did not call the technical foul. With 0:00 on the clock, the Suns should have received a technical foul shot—Westphal likely would have shot it—to try to win the game. But Phoenix never got the chance because Powers failed to acknowledge Silas's obvious—and blatant —call for a timeout.

"It was not a smart play on my part," Silas admitted in the *Globe*.

"Richie was looking right at him and chose not to call it," said Westphal.

"I thought Phoenix got screwed," said Rick Barry. "Richie Powers said, 'I chose to ignore his request.' That's exactly what he said. What the hell was that? That's your job. It would've been a technical foul, and Paul Westphal probably would've gone to the line and made the free throw, and that would've been the end of the game. It was horrendous. I felt badly for Phoenix because they got hosed. That was ridiculous."

Said John MacLeod in the *Globe*, "[Richie] didn't want Boston to lose. Westphal would have made the technical foul [shot] and we would have won, and we would have won Game 6. I'm still angry. How many chances do you get to win a championship?"

"We very easily could've won it right there," Awtrey said. "Frankly, though, it didn't bother me particularly. Richie should've called the timeout, but things happen. The only thing that bothered me later was that I heard three different excuses for why Richie didn't call the technical foul. If he would've said, 'I'm not going to make the call that might cost them the championship,' I can understand that a little bit. But if you start hemming and hawing about why you didn't do it, that really bothers me. Looking back on it, it was upsetting. At that point, you just play."

"Richie Powers may have taken an early NBA championship away from the Phoenix Suns," said Al McCoy. "Afterwards, he said he didn't want to see an NBA championship decided by a call like that. Well, I didn't know that referees were there to make the rules. I thought they were there to enforce them."

"That was as close as I ever came to winning a championship," said Van Arsdale in the *Globe*. "I would [have been happy winning that way]. I would have taken that."

"About two weeks later," said Jerry Colangelo in the same article, "a local Phoenix golf pro named Joe Porter was playing in the Westchester Classic [now the Northern Trust, in the New York area]. He saw Richie Powers at the bar and he asked him why he didn't call the timeout. He says that Richie said, 'I didn't want Boston to lose like that.' If you ask me 25 years later do I think he meant 'I didn't want *anyone* to lose like that' or '*Boston* to lose like that,' I'll say the latter."

Added Wetzel, "It was one of those things that we, as players and coaches, have no control over. It was wrong. It was one of those things that … it's been stuck in our craw for 45 years."

"Richie Powers saw it, but he ignored Silas. It was unbelievable," Kuberski said.

"You hate to think that somebody would do that on purpose. It's pretty pathetic. It's very sad," said Keith Erickson, who suffered a high ankle sprain early in the first quarter and spent the rest of the game in the locker room.

Alternate referee Bob Rakel took a different—and predictable—stance. "That is good refereeing," he told the *Globe*. "You don't want to end a contest like that under those circumstances. Now, if Silas had kept coming back [to Powers], that might be different."

Said Al Bianchi, "After all my years with Syracuse and then Philadelphia, and getting our asses beat up in Boston, it was like, 'When the hell are we going to get rid of these demons in the Boston Garden?' When we went to Philadelphia the next season, I knew a jeweler there, and I told him I need a ring that says, '1975–76 Phoenix Suns NBA Champs.' On the inside, I told him to put an inscription that says, 'Fuck you, Richie Powers.' I still wear the ring to this day."

Colangelo was sitting at midcourt, opposite the two benches when the whole thing went down. "It was 90-plus degrees in the building. It was near midnight, and the intensity was over the top," he said. "Coulda been, woulda been, shoulda been ... that's yesterday's news."

Perry had a relatively healthy outlook of the situation. "Even though it was obvious Richie Powers didn't acknowledge the timeout call by Silas, we can't say, 'The referees did this, the referees did that,'" he said. "The game was going into overtime, and that was what we had to deal with. We couldn't sit there and whine about what could've been or 'if this' or 'maybe that.' We had to stay in the moment ... 'let's get 'em in overtime!'"

BEYOND BELIEF

The Suns were a confident bunch. "We actually felt like we could beat [Boston] in the first overtime, especially once we came from 20 [actually 22] down," said Gar Heard in *Awesome Endings*.

Even though there was no television in the Phoenix locker room, the injured Keith Erickson could tell what was going on out on the court. "Early in the fourth quarter, the Celtics' ball boys brought in our warmups to put away," he said in the *Globe*. "They were smiling and laughing because they thought the Celtics were in control. At the start of the overtime, they came in to get them again. They were very somber. It was interesting being in that room. The Garden was like an old tin can. I could feel the ebb and flow of the game. It was like waves breaking on top of you when you're underwater."

Recalled Joe Proski, the Suns' trainer, in the same article, "Fans are yelling at [Al] Bianchi and he's yelling back. They were right in the huddle. John [MacLeod] would be drawing up a play and a fan would yell, 'That's not gonna work!'"

Boston got things started in overtime when Paul Silas tipped in a missed jumper by Don Nelson. A few moments later, Dave Cowens's jumper from the top of the circle gave the Celtics a 99–95 lead. Phoenix cut its deficit to two points with 2:10 to go when Heard hit a high, arching jumper from the lane. Jo Jo White swished a long, open jumper from the left baseline to give the home team a 101–97 advantage, but then Curtis Perry banked in a beautiful turnaround jumper with Nelson guarding him to make it 101–99. A few moments later, Heard connected from the left baseline with John Havlicek guarding him to tie the game at 101 with 45 seconds remaining. Those were the last points of the first extra period. Overtime number two was next.

White got things started in the second overtime when he swished a jumper from the left baseline to put Boston up, 103–101. Following a Celtics turnover, Ricky Sobers drove for an uncontested layup to even the score. White hit a wide-open jumper from the right but Sobers responded by knocking down a fadeaway jumper from the right baseline in which he was fouled by Nelson. He made the free throw as Phoenix forged ahead, 106–105. Cowens missed a short bank shot from the lane but was fouled by Dennis Awtrey, causing fury across the Suns bench. Cowens converted both free throws as Boston retook the lead, 107–106.

After two possession exchanges, the visitors called a timeout with 1:33 left. Sobers missed a long jumper. Then Cowens, despite being triple-teamed, sank a jumper from the right baseline but was called for an offensive foul, bumping Awtrey, fouling out with one minute to go. Heard missed a jumper from the free throw line. While positioning for the rebound, Awtrey fouled Havlicek and fouled out himself with 38 ticks on the clock. He was visibly upset at the call. "As I was going up for the rebound, Paul Silas pushed me about four feet in the air, and I landed on somebody else," he said. "With Alvan having already fouled out earlier, we didn't have anybody else who knew how to play center really. Curtis moved in to play the center position."

On Boston's next possession, White dribbled to the right and, with his right hand, threw the ball up over Heard's outstretched right arm and banked it in. The Celtics' lead was now 109–106 with 19 seconds remaining.

This is where the real fireworks began.

After a Phoenix timeout, Heard inbounded the ball to Dick Van Arsdale, who dribbled to the left and swished a jumper from the left baseline, pulling the Suns to within one point at 109–108 with 15 seconds left. Jim Ard tried to inbound the ball to Havlicek, but Paul Westphal came out of nowhere to knock it away, then saved it from going out of bounds by, while falling out of bounds, passing the ball to Van Arsdale. Van Arsdale quickly threw it to Perry, who missed a wide-open jumper from the left. Havlicek got his left hand on the ball while trying for the rebound, but instead knocked it back to Perry, who, with Havlicek guarding him, pump faked and then swished a jumper from the left baseline. Incredibly, Phoenix now had the lead, 110–109, with five seconds to go.

"When I saw the ball come off the backboard, it bounced out pretty far," said Perry. "When Havlicek tipped it, I just grabbed it. I was tuned in and knew how much time was on the clock, so I had time to give him a little fake just in case he wanted to foul me. Then I shot the ball, and I had no doubt that it was going in."

"The pump fake, for some reason, enabled me to get my rhythm. The shot was easy," Perry said in the *Globe*.

According to Steve Kuberski, "Curtis wasn't even a good outside shooter."

Boston called timeout.

The tension in the Garden could be cut with a knife.

In the Phoenix huddle, John MacLeod told his players not to foul anybody who was shooting the ball. Nelson inbounded the ball to Havlicek. He dribbled to the left and banked in a running jumper, an extremely difficult shot, as the Celtics forged back ahead, 111–110.

"I said to myself, 'I'm going to split the gap, flail my elbows, and hope they foul me," Havlicek recalled in the *Globe*. "But I'm sure MacLeod was telling them not to foul, because Sobers backed off and the gap actually got bigger."

"The guy we were most concerned about was Havlicek, and we wanted to have help, and I'll be a son of a gun if he didn't break loose," MacLeod said in *Awesome Endings*.

"The shot Havlicek made was exactly the shot John [MacLeod] said in the huddle that they were going to take," said Bianchi. "He said, 'They're going to give it to Havlicek. Chase him left and make sure he doesn't go to the right.' And, I'll be a son of a bitch, our players did exactly what they were supposed to do, and he made an unbelievable shot that great players do."

"When [Havlicek] left his feet, everybody backed off. He put it off the board. I don't know if his feet came down or not, but that was a hell of a shot," Perry told the *Globe*.

In that same article, Bianchi said, "He almost shattered the glass."

"He was not afraid to make a move in the clutch," Red Auerbach said in an NBA TV video. "A lot of ballplayers, they don't want that last shot. Not John. 'Give it to me.' He'll take it."

"He was a great scorer," said Tom Heinsohn in the same video. "He was a winner in every sense of the word … loved the pressure situations, loved to come through."

"A lot of the fans were all beered up already before they *got* to the game, and they were just waiting … waiting to explode," laughed John Wetzel. "And they did."

After Havlicek gave Boston that one-point lead, the clock ran out, and hundreds of crazed Celtics fans rushed the court to celebrate what they thought was a one-point victory. "I thought it was a very slow clock when Boston put the ball in play," Jerry Colangelo remembered. "It seemed as though five seconds went by before Havlicek took the shot, and they didn't have that much time. But after he made the shot, I knew there was something left on the clock, I just didn't know what."

"Red had those guys [timekeepers] trained," said Westphal.

"We left the floor right away and went into the dressing room, thinking the game was over," said Kuberski.

"Red taught us to do that," Nelson said in the *Globe*. "We were taught, 'Don't wait or hang around. Make it hard on the officials. Put the pressure on them.' It was a tactic that had worked before many times."

"We were cheering and excited and giving each other high fives because we thought we'd won," said Glenn McDonald.

While Richie Powers and Don Murphy, the other referee, were deciding if any time should be put back on the clock, Boston fans continued to take over the court, yelling and dancing and jumping around.

"It was a mess there for a couple minutes," said Wetzel.

"We were trying to get time put back on the clock because Boston's timekeeper had a green thumb," Perry laughed.

It was announced that one second would be put back on the clock. "There should've been at least two seconds put back on," Westphal said. "But the refs did have enough courage to put some time back on the clock."

One fan was so incensed that a second was put back on the clock, he attacked Powers!

"It was bizarre, incredible," said Bob Ryan. "I'd never seen anything like it before and haven't since. Who has? It was crazy. Security was nothing like it is now. In fact, the Suns were very adamant that the security in Boston was horrible. There wasn't any protection. It was scary. I remember distinctly, going back to the Kareem hook in the Milwaukee game in the '74 finals, that the fans were massing around the court and around the scorers' table. Had the game ended with a Boston victory after Havlicek's shot, they were coming, and they were coming over the top, and I had to clutch my typewriter to protect it. That's the way it was for Game 5."

"That still is the single most amazing thing about that game to me," Heard said in the *Globe* story. "A fan attacked the referee!"

In the same article, Bob Rakel called the situation "[F]rightening. I was sitting there right in the middle of all of them [at half court] and I was hoping they wouldn't come after me [they didn't]."

"I ended up out on the middle of the floor," remembered Wetzel. "That fan and Richie Powers were duking it out, and I kind of grabbed the guy from behind to try to help Richie. I think the guy was swinging at him, and I didn't want Richie to get beat up. It looked like it was out of a Laurel and Hardy movie. It was the only time I got off the bench that night."

"All of a sudden," said Awtrey, "I think we've got a couple players in the middle of the scrum there, so I chased on through, pulling people out of the way, to get to protect my teammates. I saw they had Richie, and I said, 'Oh, screw it, go ahead.' Instead of going to protect Richie, I decided I was going to protect my teammates and not protect him. I wasn't nearly as concerned about him as I was about my own teammates."

"Curtis Perry got the guy off of Richie Powers," Al McCoy recalled. "He kept him from getting beat up! Later on, Curtis said he should've let him punch out Richie because of what happened at the end of regulation."

"Curtis saved [Powers's] life, because this guy was *serious*," remembered Ricky Sobers in the *Globe*.

Said Perry in the same story, "People keep asking me, 'Why did I save Richie Powers?' because I had no love for him. It was because I sure didn't like the alternate [Rakel]!"

"My broadcast position was off the floor a little bit, and a Boston fan passed out right in my lap while I was on the air!" McCoy recalled. "And I realized that this broadcast may be tougher than I thought. I was eventually able to get the guy off my lap."

"Those fans gave us a chance to regroup," Heard told the *Globe*. "Had it been the normal flow of the game, we wouldn't have had a chance to stop and think about it. But we all returned to talk things over."

Word was sent to the Boston locker room that one second was put back on the clock. "All of a sudden," said McDonald, "there was the disappointment aspect of when they came into the locker room and told us we had to come back out to the court because the game wasn't over."

"Guys were taking tape off their ankles and this and that," Kuberski said. "When we were called out to the court, a lot of guys didn't even bother to get them retaped, thinking, 'There's only one second left. What are they gonna do?'"

"We didn't think they'd have the guts to bring us back out, but they did," Nelson said in the *Globe*.

"It was pretty wild," said Kevin Stacom.

In the midst of all the mayhem going on out on the basketball court, the wheels were spinning in Paul Westphal's mind. A thinking man's player, he called a timeout even though Phoenix didn't have any left. He did this purposely so a technical foul would be called on him. Although the Celtics got a free throw attempt, the Suns would get the ball at midcourt instead of having to go the entire length of the floor. "I got the idea from watching a lot of USC football games," said Westphal in the *Globe*. "John McKay's teams had a lot of comebacks, and I remember him calling timeouts when they didn't have any, and the penalty wasn't much, five yards or something. The punishment didn't fit the crime, and I figured basketball might be the same way. I asked Richie what would happen if we called time, and he said, 'You don't have any.' I said, 'But what if we *do* [call timeout]? And he told me. So I said, 'All right, timeout, then.'

"Talking to the official, I said my understanding of the rule is that we'd be able to advance the ball to half-court if we called the illegal timeout. And he said, 'Yeah.' So I called it and then went over and told John what I did, and he was good with it. He had fans climbing all over him, so he couldn't really deal with the conversation I was having with the official at the time in order to call a timeout."

"Heads up call by Westphal to call the timeout and give us the technical [free throw]," said Cowens in *Awesome Endings.*

"How smart that was. They got to advance the ball," added Nelson in the *Globe* story.

Said Colangelo, "Thank goodness Paul Westphal called that timeout and that he had the foresight of knowing that, yes, it would be a technical, but more importantly, you'd get the ball at half-court. It was a brilliant decision."

"Having Paul Westphal was like having another coach on the floor," said McCoy. "It was almost impossible to have a timeout because the fans were right there. There was no security in that building at all. Coach MacLeod had to bring the huddle way out on the floor!"

"Westphal figured it out," Ryan said. "He went up to the table and asked them what happens if he calls time. You can see him on the video just gesturing and pointing to the clock and the table and MacLeod. It was a very rare situation."

Said Adams, "Paul being the master gamesman he is, whether he's playing Monopoly or whatever, he had that in his bag of tricks."

"Paul always had a great offensive mind," said Bianchi of the gentleman who, 17 years later, would lead the Suns to the NBA Finals in his first season as their head coach.

Because of Westphal's quick thinking, the "Westphal Rule" was put in the next season, meaning that a team must have to have a timeout left in order to advance the ball to midcourt after a basket by the other team.

"I didn't want to get a technical arguing," said Heinsohn in the *Globe* story. "All we'd have to do was defend a very difficult shot."

First things first. White sank the technical foul shot to give Boston a 112–110 lead.

"The Boston fans were crazy, but they are some of the most knowledgeable fans," Adams said. "I never heard anybody say anything stupid about the game there. They may have said something abusive, but they never said anything stupid. People had been drinking, and people were crowded around the court. I remember it being crazy. When they put the one second back on the clock, we, of course, didn't have tenths of a second on the clock back then, so when there was a one put back up there, you're thinking, 'Is that 1.9 or is it .1?' You know in Boston, as soon as the opponent inbounds the ball, the guy is going to push the buzzer, and it's going to go off."

"You can feel the tension in the Garden start picking up and picking up," said Heard in *Awesome Endings*.

"We had a two-option play," said MacLeod in the same video. "One was designed for Paul Westphal down in the corner, and the other option was for Curtis Perry to throw the ball into Garfield Heard up at the top of the key."

From midcourt on the right, Perry inbounded the ball to Heard just beyond the top right of the circle. With his back to the basket, Heard turned to his left, and with Nelson guarding him, lifted a high-arching, rainbow shot into the air as the clock ran out. The ball fell through the basket, tying the score, 112–112, and forcing a third overtime. It was incredible!

"The first option was Westphal because he was our scorer," said Heard. "I knew I was the second option. I'd played for John in college, and I'd made a couple shots for him in college. We figured that Westphal was going to be covered. Don Nelson was on me, and he was not a shot blocker, so I knew I could get the shot off if I got the ball. Curtis couldn't get the ball to Westphal, but he found me at the top of the key, and I ended up making the shot. That rainbow shot was my shot. I knew I could get it up in the air. That's the type of shot you dream about making. As a kid when you're just shooting around by yourself, you say, 'This is for the championship.' And I had the opportunity to take that shot, and luckily it went in. When the shot went in, I never thought about it going down as one of the most memorable shots in NBA history. At that time, we had a chance to win the game. I really thought we were going to win the game after that shot."

"There wasn't a soul in the United States who didn't figure the ball was going to go to Westphal," said Perry. "And, if he was covered, Gar was going to blast to the top of the key. So, when I got the ball, Don Nelson trailed Gar up to the top of the key because he figured it was going to Westphal. Westphal was covered, and they were ready for that pass. So when Gar broke to the top of the key to draw the defense out, Nelson trailed him up there behind him, and I had a clear path for a pass, and I was able to give Gar a good pass. When the ball went in the net, I knew we were going to beat them then—'We got 'em, we got 'em now.'"

"[Heard] caught it, turned, and shot. I got a hand up, but he really had an arc on that shot," Nelson recalled in the *Globe*.

Said Heard in the same article, "I never thought I'd have the chance in Boston Garden with all those leprechauns."

"Moon Rock, that's what I call it," said Ricky Sobers in the *Globe*. "I tease him all the time that it was the only jump shot he made all year."

Also in the *Globe*, Perry called it "Gar's aurora borealis shot."

"God, it was fabulous … to knock that thing down," said Awtrey. "Talk about a clutch play for a guy who wasn't a great shooter."

"It was unbelievable," laughed McCoy. "What I screamed was, 'It's up and good, and I have to tell you, somebody up there must be on our side!"

"I went, 'Wow! Give me a break,'" Heinsohn remembered. "Don Nelson was right there with [Heard]. He wasn't going to foul him. He had his hands up, he challenged the shot … it was a catch, turn, and shoot, and it went in. It wasn't an easy shot, but he did it! Those are the situations where you just take your hat off to the guy and say, 'Nice job.'"

According to Searcy, there was nothing to say. He said that everybody was just stunned and that Heinsohn basically said, "You just have to buckle up."

"That shot is engraved in everyone's mind," Rakel said in the *Globe*.

Jim Ard thought the game was over and that the Celtics had lost. "I forgot about Jo Jo hitting the [technical] free throw," he said. "Then Paul [Silas] said to me, 'Wait, hold on. That only *tied* the game."

"It was just one of those situations where all the air goes out right then because now you know this is going to a third overtime," McDonald said. "Then you just have to prepare your mind for a third overtime."

"In retrospect, because of the nature of that game, we probably should've expected that shot to go in," said Ryan. "The game had already established itself for so many interesting, intriguing ways. When Heard's shot went in, I probably said, 'Oh shit' on two levels—one, I'm obviously wanting the Celtics to win and two, 'Oh my God, we've got to get going here.' We writers were worried about our deadlines. The game ended at 12:08 a.m. The biggest deadline was somewhere around 11:30, so we missed that one. It was only going to be a case of getting it into the final edition."

"When it happened, you almost felt like this was destiny," said Colangelo. "But I also knew that we had given up a lot of energy just coming back. We had to come from way back, so going into that third overtime, you may have felt you were confident, but you were also exhausted."

"When Gar hit that shot, we were all excited, thinking, 'We've got a chance to win this thing!'" Wetzel declared. "We thought that fate was on our side. We felt really good about it. Going into that third overtime, we thought we were going to have a chance to pull off an upset."

Added Bianchi, "Even with Alvan on the bench, I thought maybe we'd be able to win the game."

10

IT'S NOT OVER TILL IT'S OVER

As Phoenix and Boston were about to embark upon a third overtime in this already remarkable Game 5 of the 1976 NBA Finals, Brent Musburger and Rick Barry made it known on CBS's telecast just how impressed they were with the amazing guts and determination of the Suns and Celtics players.

"You play 58 minutes of basketball and have to go five more minutes this late in the season ... that's an incredible feat," said Barry. "And I think right now, coming down to a situation where you're going to have this game decided by men who are not the top stars perhaps ... Dave Cowens sitting on the bench, Charlie Scott on the bench, Alvan Adams on the bench ... absolutely incredible. This is *some* basketball game right here, ladies and gentlemen. You are seeing a fantastic effort by both ballclubs, something that you can remember for the rest of your life."

"You talk about pressure situations," Musburger said. "You play 48 minutes. Then you play 10 minutes of overtime ... you've got men going up and down the court. I honestly don't know how these athletes can stand the tension and the pressure of this game. It is a tribute to every man in the NBA what's happening here tonight at the Boston Garden. Now we come to the third overtime of, by far, the most incredible basketball game I've ever witnessed."

Phoenix won the opening tip of the third overtime, but Dick Van Arsdale traveled, giving the ball to Boston. A few moments later, Don Nelson banked in a jumper from the left to give the Celtics a 114–112 lead. The Suns tied the game when Ricky Sobers laid the ball in off a nice pass from Curtis Perry. John Havlicek then missed a jumper from out front.

While Gar Heard went for the rebound, he was fouled by Paul Silas, who fouled out.

"When Paul fouled out," remembered Glenn McDonald, "I tapped Steve [Kuberski] because that's the position he played—power forward—and told him, 'Get ready to go in.' But then, all of a sudden, Tom [Heinsohn] hollers, 'Mac, get in there!' So I jumped up and went in the game. Tommy knew that I was pretty fresh. He wanted me to get out there and basically run. Whoever was going to be guarding me, run them to death. That way, I could probably get some easy shots."

The sweat was dripping from every player on the court. "You have to realize, in that old Boston Garden there was no air conditioning. It was an unusually hot day in Boston that day," recalled Al McCoy. "It was so hot, guys were even having problems getting up and down the floor. It was a tough scenario. Nobody had any real juice at all. Glenn McDonald and Jim Ard were the only guys on the floor who had any energy!"

Phoenix took a 116–114 lead when Perry hit a jumper from the right. Havlicek responded with a nice pass inside to Jo Jo White, who drove for a wide-open layup to tie the score. Heard gave the Suns a 118–116 lead with 2:47 remaining when he swished a rainbow jumper from the left baseline with Ard guarding him. Two turnovers later, White canned a jumper from the left to tie the score at 118. A few moments later, White drove towards the basket on the left but was met there by Van Arsdale, so he passed the ball to McDonald on the right. McDonald banked in a short jumper to put Boston back on top, 120–118, with 1:39 to go. John MacLeod wanted a timeout, but no one saw him. Heard missed a jumper from the left, and the ball was batted to Don Nelson. Several passes later, Havlicek threw the ball inside to McDonald on the left baseline. McDonald sank a short turnaround, fadeaway jumper with Van Arsdale guarding him. The Celtics now had a 122–118 lead with 1:14 left.

"Havlicek," said McDonald, "had been working with me forever on that shot, how to catch, turn, pivot, and then go up with the shot, so I felt extremely comfortable when I turned and took the shot."

"That baseline shot by McDonald was a tough one," Bob Ryan said. "It was a very difficult shot."

"I don't how he made it," said White in the *Globe* article.

After a Phoenix timeout, Van Arsdale inbounded the ball to Westphal, who dribbled to the right, turned around with Havlicek guarding him, and banked in a turnaround, fadeaway shot to pull the Suns within 122–120 with 1:09 remaining. White responded by connecting on a wide-open jumper from the left for a four-point Boston lead. Van Arsdale then missed a jumper from the left baseline with White guarding him. McDonald rebounded the ball, dribbled, and was fouled by Perry with 36 seconds to go. By this time, White was so exhausted that he sat down in the backcourt while everyone else was walking up the floor for McDonald's free throw attempts, as the Celtics were in the bonus. McDonald sank both free throws to increase the Boston lead to 126–120.

"Those six points McDonald scored during that minute-plus period were crucial," said Ryan.

"Those were the biggest shots of the game. We knew the other guys. This kid came into the game and made those shots. It was devastating," Al Bianchi said in the *Globe*.

"I wasn't nervous at all because the adrenaline was running," said McDonald. "Every time I went to the free throw line I said, 'I'll make this free throw, I'll make this free throw.' And, in that situation, I said the same thing for the first free throw. And when the second free throw came, I said it again. I wasn't nervous one bit until I got home after the game and said, 'What the hell did I just do?'"

"The unlikeliest guy, Glenn McDonald, comes into the game and did what he did," said Kuberski. "I don't know what Tommy saw, but it turned out to be a great move."

"I thought he could do the job, but I didn't expect him to do what he did," Heinsohn admitted in the *Globe*.

Said Kuberski in the same article, "Glenn was a good practice player, but he would tense up in games. For him to be put into a game as intense as this and do what he did was unbelievable."

"Glenn was a lifesaver in that game," added Scott. "He came in and did a great job. We had a lot of confidence in the guys who were on our bench, guys like Glenn, Jim Ard, and Kevin Stacom. Basketball is a game of matchups, and we felt like our starting five was better than Phoenix's starting five, and we also felt that our bench players were better than their bench players."

"I've been kicking myself for 25 years that I didn't sub in [the fast] Nate Hawthorne to guard McDonald," said MacLeod in the *Globe*.

"I'm glad to hear John say that," Hawthorne said in the same article. "Each year, when this game comes on TV, I tell my wife, 'He [McDonald] never would have scored those baskets if I were in there.'"

Following the Suns' final timeout, Van Arsdale inbounded the ball to Sobers on the right. Sobers drove toward the middle of the lane and laid it in to cut the Phoenix deficit to 126–122. Nelson called a timeout when he couldn't find anyone open to inbound the ball to. After the timeout, he inbounded the ball to Havlicek on the right, but an intentional foul was called on the Suns, sending Ard, not the best free throw shooter, to the line with 31 seconds left. Recalled Ard, "Ricky Sobers asked me [sarcastically], 'Do you think you can do it?' And I said, 'Hey, I wouldn't be here if they didn't think I could make 'em,' I wasn't nervous at all, not at all. Before the playoffs started, I was practicing free throws a lot to be prepared, and sure enough, they fouled me." Ard converted both free throws, and the Celtics had a 128–122 lead.

The Suns refused to die, however.

Westphal dribbled the ball up the court, drove to the left, spun around in the air—a complete 360—and banked in an unbelievable shot with 25 seconds to go to make the score 128–124. "Paul could get a shot off at 3 a.m. in a rainstorm," said Perry in the *Globe*.

"At that point in time, Paul was the guy who always wanted the ball," said Dennis Awtrey. "He always tried to get a little edge. He was the perfect guy to take those clutch shots. He had enough confidence that he didn't worry if he missed. If he misses it, he misses it. He took the responsibility on himself and had the confidence that, 'Hey, I can do this!'"

"Westphal was terrific," Bianchi said.

"Of course, Westphal had played with Boston the three previous seasons, so he had a certain comfort level there," said Adams. "He had a real comfort level whenever he had the ball in his hands, but especially at the Boston Garden. So it wasn't a surprise that he was producing right and left, and at both ends of the floor."

Nelson inbounded the ball to White, who dribbled around while being double-teamed, then passed the ball to Havlicek on the left. Havlicek brought the ball up the court, then threw it to Ard in the left corner. Ard hooked a pass to McDonald under the basket, but he couldn't control the ball. Sobers grabbed it and immediately heaved it the length of the court to Westphal, who easily laid it in with 12 seconds to go. The Suns were within two points. Havlicek inbounded the ball to McDonald, who passed it back to Havlicek, who threw a bounce pass to Nelson on the left. Nelson dribbled once, then threw the ball up the court to Ard on the left, but Westphal—who else?—got a hand on it. His momentum carried him out of bounds, however. Ard dribbled twice, then passed the ball to White on the right. White dribbled around as the clock finally ran out. Hundreds of Celtics fans rushed the court to celebrate this amazing Boston victory. And this time, there was no doubt that the game was over.

The final score: Boston 128, Phoenix 126.

"I had my fingertips on it. I felt the ball. I just couldn't get my hand on it," Westphal recalled in the *Globe*.

"He *almost* got it," said Ard in the same article. "I was worried about two things. The first was him getting it. The second was me traveling because I had to reach so far to get it. I just wanted to get it over to Jo Jo before he fouled me."

"I'd been sitting for so long at that point … some of those guys played 60-plus minutes," Adams said. "I remember even thinking, *Okay, this is the end of the third overtime. The scoreboard says Boston is ahead, but I bet there will be a fourth overtime the way this has gone.* But it finally hit me. You kind of morphed your way back through the crowd, and they had that great entrance right there at center court. Most teams enter off the ends these days."

"It was one of those things where we just couldn't quite pull it off," said John Wetzel.

"It was big shot after big shot after big shot after big play after big play after big play," Perry said. "We didn't give up. You had to beat us, and they did."

Said Jerry Colangelo, "The pressure of the game, the heat in the building, the circumstances, took a toll on just about every player on the court. We just ran out of fuel."

"It was a blue-collar team," MacLeod told the *Globe*. "We weren't even supposed to be there. It was supposed to be a Celtics-Golden State final. They were guys who accepted coaching and worked their tails off."

"To the credit of our players, they never gave up," MacLeod said in *Awesome Endings*. "I'll say one thing about that '76 team – they refused to quit."

White scored 33 points and had nine assists and six rebounds. Cowens had 26 points and 19 rebounds. Havlicek scored 22 points and had nine rebounds and eight assists, while Silas totaled 17 points and 14 boards. McDonald and Ard wound up scoring eight points apiece.

Sobers and Westphal each scored 25 points for the Suns. Sobers added six assists. Perry was a monster with 23 points, 15 rebounds, and six assists, while Adams contributed 20 points, nine rebounds, and five assists. Heard scored 17 points and pulled down a dozen rebounds.

"When we had those leads, we just couldn't hold on," said Heard. "I think it was one of those situations where we just didn't have enough to finish them off."

"So many guys made incredible shots under intense pressure," White said in the *Globe*.

Said Perry in the same article, "Everybody who played in this game made at least one big play – and that just doesn't happen."

"All of our emotion was exhausted," Wetzel said. "The locker room was quiet. Hardly anything was said. You could just see that all of our emotion had been drained out of us. You play your heart out for that many minutes, and you come away with a loss … it's devastating! The players were exhausted."

"When the game ended," said Ard, "my teammates and I were physically and emotionally drained."

So was Heinsohn.

"Heinsohn was a very intense coach," said Stacom. "The poor guy … he struggled with his weight. His blood pressure was at its limit. I didn't even know if he was going to survive the game."

"When we got into the locker room, they asked me a question, and I was sitting there, and all of a sudden I fainted. I was totally dehydrated," Heinsohn said. "They took me to the hospital and weren't going to let me coach in Game 6 on Sunday because they were concerned that I might have a heart attack or something."

"Red [Auerbach] came into the locker room … and said, 'Don't get too upset with the referees. Get dressed and go home. You're going to be important on Sunday," recalled Scott in the *Globe*. "He and Jo Jo calmed me down. I was a very emotional player. I was unhappy because I had fouled out of five straight games, and I didn't think I was fouling that much."

Said Havlicek in the same article, "I honestly never thought they could beat us, that even if we lost Game 5, we'd still win the series."

"I remember Gar and I were sitting in the locker room after the game," said Perry. "It's not like we were going over the game. We were just kind of looking at each other."

"After the game, I went into the Phoenix locker room, and the visitor's locker room in the Boston Garden was about as bad as it could get," remembered McCoy. "There were nails for the players to hang their clothes on, and the showers had cold water. Jerry Colangelo came in and said to the players, 'Hey, we're walking out of here with our heads up high. We've got nothing to be ashamed of about this game tonight.' And there were all kinds of fans roaming around, and he said, 'If any fan gives you any trouble, you do whatever you want to do.' So we're all walking out of the locker room together, and here's Red in front of the Boston locker room smoking a cigar. Colangelo looked at him and said, 'Red, why don't you get some security in this building?' And Red said, 'Aw, I thought it was great!'"

"Everybody was mentally and emotionally drained," Bianchi said. "We win that game, we go back home and win the series in six."

Said Adams, "We were a little down but were thinking, 'Too bad we didn't win this game, but we're going to go back to Phoenix for Game 6. And, hey, we haven't lost too many games at home in the last month. Let's get back and win that one so we can get to a Game 7 back here in Boston. And how exciting will that one be?'"

THE AFTERMATH

Even though the Suns lost that unbelievable Game 5, it had a tremendous effect on the greater Phoenix area. "Without a doubt, that game galvanized our community like nothing had ever done," said Jerry Colangelo in the *Globe*.

"No single game in the history of the franchise did more to get the Suns national recognition than that loss. The impact was *immediate*. Nothing else ever did so much for them than that," said Joe Gilmartin, author of the book *The Little Team That Could ... and Darn Near Did! The Fabulous Rise of the Phoenix Suns*, in the same *Globe* article.

Less than 40 hours after Game 5 ended, Game 6 began, on Sunday, June 6 at 12:30 p.m. Mountain Standard Time.

"It was horrible scheduling. It was bad for us and for the Celtics," Paul Westphal said. "To have one day to fly across country and then play the next day, and it was an afternoon game! They should never schedule that kind of thing in the NBA Finals where you don't have a little bit of time to rest and get across country."

"We fly home Saturday and get home Saturday afternoon sometime," said John Wetzel. "We've got to be at the gym at 10 o'clock the next morning or something like that."

Game 6 was fairly close throughout, but the Suns just didn't seem to have that spark they had two nights earlier. "I think there was a little hangover from what happened in Game 5 on Friday night," Dennis Awtrey said. "We came out just a little bit flat and not charged up as much as we should've been. We just didn't respond like we would've liked to."

Even the Phoenix fans were not their typically crazed selves. "It was almost like [Game 5] took more out of the fans than it did the players," said trainer Joe Proski in the *Globe*.

Ricky Sobers agreed. "That was eerie," he said in the same article.

The game was tied, 20–20, after the first quarter. Boston led, 38–33, at halftime. Phoenix cut its deficit to 57–56 after three quarters. The Suns held a couple of brief leads in the second half, but the Celtics went on to win, 87–80, for the franchise's 13th NBA championship.

Charlie Scott scored 25 points and had 11 rebounds and five steals, while Dave Cowens had 21 points and 17 rebounds. For Phoenix, Alvan Adams scored 20 points and had nine rebounds and six assists. Sobers had 19 points and six boards.

"I think that emotion that we were drained of from Game 5, we never got it back for the next game," said Wetzel. "Whoever won the fifth game was going to win the series because, had Boston lost Game 5, they would've been spent emotionally just like we were. You prepared the same way for Game 6 as you did for Game 5, but before the game and coming out for warmups, we just didn't have … it wasn't there. We couldn't get back up, couldn't get the emotional high again."

"I suppose we might've been mentally exhausted from the game on Friday night," Adams said. "Did we run out of steam? Did we run out of magic? Did the Celtics just kick it up a notch? I don't remember them kicking it up a notch. I thought we were a little flat, for whatever reason."

"I think Game 6 was a case of fatigue," said Heard. "The guy who had the best game was Charlie Scott, who fouled out before the overtimes in Game 5."

Said Al Bianchi, "I think there was somewhat of a letdown, but I think that, with the group we had, they just tried so hard, and sometimes when you do that, you start to press a little bit."

"After the triple-overtime game, no one slept. Everybody was up all night in the hotel," Al McCoy recalled. "And we had about a 7 o'clock flight, and we came back to Phoenix. It had been such an emotional loss that it was just tough to get back and going again, and what happened Sunday happened. It was back and forth, and the Suns had some runs, and it looked like they might be able to do it, but they were never really able to finish Boston off. They just kind of seemed to be spent."

"Down the stretch, about halfway through the fourth quarter, we kind of took control," said Steve Kuberski. "I think emotionally the Suns just didn't have anything left. They overachieved. Nobody thought they were going to do that well."

Perry took a somewhat different stance. "I don't think we let down. They just beat us," he said. "You're not going to have two greatest games ever played in a row. I don't make excuses. Boston beat us. They didn't beat us by much, but they won the game."

"I think Dave and Charlie, and Jo Jo too, were going to play the whole game [the starters all played at least 40 minutes] no matter what, and they were going to win," said Jim Ard. "I think the stoneheadedness of the players said, 'We just aren't going to lose.'"

"We just played a better game," Cowens said on *Legends with Leyden*. "We were motivated to end it, and they were motivated to keep it going."

"We eked out a title from that team," said Tom Heinsohn, who ended up fighting through his health issues, making the trip out to Phoenix, and coaching the game. "It wasn't the best team I had, but it was a gutsy team."

"The Celtics were happy when it was over," Bob Ryan said. "It was relief, not joy except for one person—Jo Jo, who was at his peak. Silas, Havlicek, Cowens, and [Don] Nelson were just glad it was over and were ready to go home."

Said Dick Van Arsdale in *Awesome Endings*, "That championship series did not mean nearly as much to the Celtics as it would've meant to the Phoenix Suns."

"[Game 5] was the start of a nice 10-year run for us. It really established us," Bianchi said in the *Globe*.

Two additions to Phoenix in 1976–77 were point guard Ron Lee and small forward Ira Terrell. Lee was a first-round draft choice out of the University of Oregon. Terrell was a third-round draft pick from Southern Methodist University.

"Ron 'The Tasmanian Devil' was just a dynamo," said Adams. "You'd just wind him up. He ate powdered sugar donuts and had a Coke before every practice. He'd take charge and he'd flop. He'd stand in front of a cement truck to take a charge. He was one of those guys who'd chase down anybody on the fast break."

"Ron was the hardest-playing guy I think I ever played against, both in practice and in a game," Westphal said. "He just went all-out every play and didn't know any fear at all about whether his body was going to take a beating or not. He'd dive into anything to try to make a play."

"There wasn't a loose ball that he didn't dive for—ever," said Colangelo. "He was a big crowd favorite because of his tenacity and willingness to give up his body."

"Ira was a really good ballplayer," said Perry. "He had a good jump shot, he moved very, very well without the ball, and he was a good passer."

"Ira would get out and run," Bianchi said. "He gave us some athleticism."

Unfortunately, Heard and Perry both missed almost half of the 1976–77 season due to injuries, and a 12-game losing streak in late February and early March doomed the Suns, who fell to 34–48 and last place in the Pacific Division.

"We had such high hopes heading into that season," said Adams.

New to Phoenix in 1977–78 were small forward Walter Davis and point guards Don Buse and Mike Bratz. Davis was the jewel of the three. He was a first-round draft choice out of the University of North Carolina. Buse was traded from the Indiana Pacers for Sobers, and Bratz was a third-round draft pick from Stanford.

"Walter came in and, from the very first day, said, 'I belong here,'" said Awtrey. "He didn't worry about 'Oh, I'm a rookie, so maybe I shouldn't do this, or I shouldn't try to take over.' He knew how good he was. I think he could've been one of the all-time greatest small forwards in the history of the league. His 15-, 17-foot shot was just incredible. Unfortunately, later on he became a big guard because of the way the team was comprised, but he was a very good big guard. As a forward, though, he was just unstoppable. They called him the 'Greyhound' because, in college, he could run a mile in less than five minutes. He was an incredible athlete."

"Walter was one of the purest jump shooters ever to play in the NBA," Colangelo said. "They called him 'Sweet D' because his jump shot was about as sweet as it could be."

"He was the greatest shooter I've ever been around," said Westphal. "His mid-range jumper was money in the bank. He made it look so easy when he scored. He was a devastating offensive player."

"Don could guard some people and could put some points up on the board," said Bianchi. "He just went out there quietly and did his job."

"He was one of the smartest ballplayers in the league," Perry said. "He was steady and made very few mistakes. He was one of the really good passers, too."

"Mike was a really good shooter, a solid backup guard who could play either guard position," said Westphal.

The Suns improved to 49–33 in 1977–78 and second place in the Pacific behind Portland. They were upset by Milwaukee, however, two games to none, in the first round of the playoffs. "*Sports Illustrated* picked us to win it all in '77–'78, and the first two-thirds of the season we really played well," Awtrey said. "But, in absolute contrast to the '75–'76 season, we went into the playoffs not playing very well. Our defense had gotten a little soft. We just didn't come into the playoffs with a lot of energy."

An eight-game winning streak late in the 1978-79 season helped Phoenix to a 50–32 record and second place again in the Pacific Division behind Seattle. Halfway through the schedule, the Suns acquired power forward Truck Robinson in a trade with the New Orleans Jazz.

"Before Truck came to Phoenix," said Adams, "we had so much trouble with guys like Elvin Hayes and Spencer Haywood. Truck came in with a lot of credentials. He was a rebounder, a scorer, just a powerful player. Once we got him on the team, we had a chance against some of those big forwards who we had trouble with before."

"Truck was very talented and versatile," said Westphal. "He was labeled as a power forward, but he could play out on the perimeter just as well. He was one of the great rebounders of his time."

"He was a big, strong, tough guy," Rick Barry said. "He'd take you, post you up, and shoot the mid-range shot."

The Suns made a deep run in the 1978–79 postseason. They ousted Portland, two games to one, in the first round and Kansas City, four games to one, in the Western Conference semifinals. In the conference finals, they led Seattle three games to two, then lost a one-point heartbreaker at home and fell, 114–110, in Game 7 at Seattle. The next season, in 1979–80, Phoenix improved to 55–27 but dropped to third place in the Pacific, much of that due to Magic Johnson joining Kareem Abdul-Jabbar in Los Angeles and leading the Lakers to a first-place finish. After defeating the Kings, two games to one, in the first round of the playoffs, the Suns were easily beaten by the Lakers in five games in the Western semifinals. Phoenix continued to be a postseason regular through 1984–85, advancing to the conference finals in 1983–84 with just a 41–41 record, reminiscent of the team's 1975–76 playoff run. Unfortunately, the Suns' opponent in the Western Conference finals was the Lakers, who ousted them in a hard-fought six-game series.

"It was one of those situations where the West got better," Heard said. "Portland had a great run with [Bill] Walton and [Maurice] Lucas and those guys. And then the Lakers had a great run with Magic and Kareem."

Said Bianchi, "I'd always say to John [MacLeod], 'LA's point guard, Magic Johnson, is bigger than our center.'"

"It's hard to get to the finals," said Westphal, who was traded to Seattle for Dennis Johnson following the 1979–80 season. "You can never take it for granted. A couple of our teams in the late 1970s were arguably better than that '76 team. If you don't take advantage of your chance when it's there in front of you, it doesn't always happen again."

After three down seasons in the late 1980s, Cotton Fitzsimmons returned as head coach in 1988–89. He helped return the Suns to prominence, but it was none other than Paul Westphal who, in his first season as a head coach, led them to the 1993 NBA Finals, where they lost to Michael Jordan and the Chicago Bulls. Phoenix qualified for the playoffs most every season all the way through 2009–10, but the franchise has experienced mainly tough times since then.

As for the Celtics in 1976–77, out was Paul Silas, who, because of a contract dispute, signed with the Denver Nuggets, and in were former UCLA teammates Sidney Wicks and Curtis Rowe. Both were power forwards. Wicks was sold by Portland to Boston. Rowe was traded from Detroit in the same deal that sent Silas to the Nuggets.

"Sidney was the guy who took Paul Silas's position, but he wasn't exactly the same type of player as Silas," said Heinsohn. "Silas was a rebounder, a defensive player, and a leader of a team, and Sidney was more a scorer than anything else. He was really effective for me his first year with us."

"Sidney was one of the greatest college players who ever lived," Bob Ryan said. "His NBA career was distinguished by diminishing returns.

His points per game diminished every year he was in the league. He was a frustrating talent. Heinsohn wanted him to be more of a rebounder and less of a shooter, but Sidney rebelled over that. His attitude with the Celtics was the antithesis of the way John Wooden had raised him at UCLA. Sidney was universally disliked and despised by the Celtics fans."

"Everybody was excited about Sidney coming to the team," recalled Steve Kuberski. "He had a couple of great games at the start, but then … I don't know if it was an attitude change or what … he just didn't seem to care emotionally about the game. There was just some spark missing.

"Curtis never fit in from the start. He was hurt on and off, never really got into it. His game certainly went downhill from when he was with Detroit."

"He might've been the ultimate mercenary," Ryan said. "You got no impression that he cared who won the game. Allegedly, a young Cedric Maxwell [a season or two later] was lamenting a loss after a game, and Rowe said to him something along the lines of, 'Don't worry about it, kid, they don't put the Ws and Ls on the paycheck.' That's a famous line that resonates in Boston. Rowe was a mediocre player."

"Our team started to disintegrate when Silas left," said Heinsohn.

"Paul was the linchpin," said Kevin Stacom. "He and Dave Cowens together were I think the best one-two punch when it comes to what big men are supposed to do in the league. It was a very unique chemistry. Paul was a winner. He did so many things to help you win ballgames."

Cowens was so upset about losing Silas, he revolted and took more than a two-month sabbatical from early November 1976 to mid-January 1977. "The whole morale of the team went south," Heinsohn said.

On top of all of that, Scott broke his wrist and missed almost half the season.

The Celtics were inconsistent in 1976–77, but a late push resulted in a 44–38 record and second place in the Atlantic Division, six games behind Philadelphia. They knocked off San Antonio, two games to none, in the first round of the playoffs before fighting to the very end in losing a tough seven-game series to the heavily favored 76ers in the Eastern Conference semifinals. "Philadelphia had Dr. J, George McGinnis, and Lloyd Free [now World B. Free]. The Celtics did very well to take them seven games," said Ryan. "I was off the beat and covering baseball then, so I was in the stands for the Celtics' Game 6 win in Boston. That series was the last hurrah for that group. Havlicek basically outplayed Dr. J all series. Jo Jo played well, too. They just didn't have it in Game 7 at Philly. I remember being in the press room at Fenway Park covering the Red Sox trying to keep track of that game. The Sixers were just the better team."

Said Scott, "Without my absence and Cowens's absence during the regular season, we might've had the seventh game against Philadelphia at home and maybe would've even won back-to-back championships."

The bottom finally fell out for the Celtics the next two seasons. Havlicek retired. Scott and White were traded. Stopping in for a cup of coffee were Dave Bing, Kermit Washington, Marvin Barnes, Billy Knight, and Bob McAdoo. There was a coaching carousel of Heinsohn, Tom Sanders, and even Cowens as a player-coach.

"The whole thing blew up because of a change in ownership," said Heinsohn. "Even Red Auerbach's career was in jeopardy!"

The Celtics dropped to 32–50 in 1977–78 and 29–53 in 1978–79.

Soon after, though, several moves got the Celtics back in the groove. In 1979, they signed forward Larry Bird, whom they had drafted in the first round out of Indiana State the year before. Also in 1979, they hired Bill Fitch as head coach. In addition, that summer the Celtics signed free agents Gerald Henderson, a point guard, and M. L. Carr, a small forward. And the great Tiny Archibald, a point guard, came back in shape in his second season with the Celtics in 1979–80 after getting traded from the San Diego Clippers in the summer of 1978 when he was out of shape.

"I was confident Bird was going to be very good," said Ryan. "I have a theory. In the history of the NBA, when you're talking about the elite of the elite players, the greatest of the greats, with the exception of two players, most turned out to be better, some much better, than people thought they were going to be. And Bird is in that category. He was far better than people projected. And he got better and better each year. By 1986, he was the best player in the world. He was a microcosm of everything that was great about basketball—the scoring, the passing, the hustle … and the brain power of seeing things before they happen.

"Gerald was one of the most finely conditioned athletes the Celtics ever had. He had speed and quickness. He was a solid individual who you were happy to have on your team. He was hardworking and a good player.

"By the time M. L. came to Boston, he was coming off a season in Detroit in which he was third in the league in minutes played. He was going to be an all-purpose sparkplug player, and he was. He was an important part of the puzzle.

"When Archibald came to Boston, he was still in recovery from his nearly career-ending Achilles problem. He wasn't the Tiny of legend. Well, in '79 he reinvented himself as a pure point guard, not as an offense-first, defense-second point guard as he was before when he led the league in scoring and assists while he was with the Kings. And he was a brilliant one. He was fantastic. He played the point guard position the way it *should* be played when he was with the Celtics."

Two other key players who were acquired during this time period were shooting guards Chris Ford and Pete Maravich. Ford was traded from Detroit early in the 1978–79 season. Maravich, who had been a legendary scorer with the Hawks and Jazz, was signed as a free agent about halfway through the 1979–80 season. One other player, Maxwell, a small forward, had been a first-round draft choice in 1977 out of the University of North Carolina at Charlotte.

"Chris wasn't very fast, but he knew how to play the game of basketball," said Ryan. "He was just a heady player."

"He could also shoot the ball," Rick Barry said. "Pete was a great player, a great showman."

"Max really knew how to play basketball," said Kevin Stacom. "He had kind of an unorthodox game. It looked like every part of his body was going in different directions. He was very difficult to guard, especially down low. He knew how to pass, move without the ball, and rebound down low. He was either going to score or get to the line or both."

"Ced could play defense, too," added Barry.

Led by Bird, plus post players Robert Parish and Kevin McHale, both of whom arrived in 1980–81, the Celtics returned to greatness, winning three more NBA titles—in 1981, 1984, and 1986. They continued to enjoy success into the early 1990s before falling on hard times for the most part through 2006–07. The next season, though, with Ray Allen and Kevin Garnett added to the team that already had Paul Pierce, Boston won the NBA title. Since then, the Celtics have been in the postseason on a regular basis.

12

THE PURPLE AND ORANGE

Paul Westphal

Paul Westphal was always a student of the game of basketball. Even when he was a player, he knew he would be a coach one day. "I always expected to get into coaching, so that was my focus after I retired from playing," he said.

Westphal the player became Westphal the "coach" with his famous timeout call that saved the day when his team, the Phoenix Suns, had none left late in the second overtime of Game 5 of the 1976 NBA Finals in Boston. Seventeen years later, in his first season as an NBA head coach. Westphal led the Suns all the way to the NBA Finals against Michael Jordan and the Chicago Bulls.

Born on November 30, 1950, in Torrance, California, Westphal grew up in nearby Redondo Beach. He played Little League baseball and organized flag football and basketball. "Baseball was my favorite sport until I got be 12 or 13 years old," he said. "In basketball, they didn't throw curveballs. I could see that I was going to be tall enough to play basketball. My older brother was a good player. I seemed to get a little better at a similar age than he had, so I could project that basketball was realistic to pursue. I was just better at basketball than those other sports. I liked the action in basketball. It was more fun. In baseball, there was too much standing around."

Westphal would play basketball with his brother and his friends. "I was always the littlest guy, but I was pretty tall for my size," he said. "I played all of the positions. I was encouraged to do that. One of the things that I think is really good for kids is to learn to play all the positions and play with people who are older and better than you. That's how you learn."

It was in fourth grade that Westphal began playing organized basketball. "I was the only fourth grader playing with the sixth graders. I played all the positions there, too," he said.

This was also the time in which Westphal's "coaching blood" first appeared. "I was the only player who knew the rules, so I didn't double dribble," he said. "Because I had an older brother, I learned the game younger than most kids my age, so I had a good head start. I just loved the game. I'd also watch it and try to learn as much as I could about how to play the game."

Westphal's junior high did not have a basketball team, so he played on a team with the best players from his area. "We played in a lot of tournaments all around Southern California," he said. "At that point, I was mostly a guard or forward. We were pretty successful. We won the title both years. We had really good teams."

As a freshman at Aviation High School, Westphal played mostly on the 'B', or junior varsity, team. "My sophomore year on the varsity team I played center, my junior year I played forward, and my senior year I played guard," he said. "We had good teams. Compton was the best high school in those days in the area. We lost to them in the postseason my junior and senior years. My junior year they just rolled over us, but my senior year we almost beast them and gave them a good game. We were arguably the second-best team in California that year."

Westphal started getting recruited by colleges after his sophomore year. "I got recruited by everybody, but I wanted to stay in Los Angeles," he said. "I was going to go to either Southern California or UCLA. "It was the hardest decision of my life. I'm not even sure to this day how I did it. I had to make a decision, that's all. I think one of the key things was that USC hadn't won at the level UCLA was winning. I thought that if we, at USC, could knock UCLA off, and if we could win at that level, it would be a bigger achievement to do it at USC as opposed to UCLA. So I think that was probably the thing that made me make up my mind, at least the biggest factor."

In 1968–69, Westphal played on the freshman team at Southern California. "We were undefeated," he said. "We had a fantastic recruiting class, and we played like it. We played up to our capabilities."

Westphal joined the varsity team his sophomore year. He averaged 14.5 points per game in helping the Trojans to an 18–8 overall record. That year, USC tied Washington State for second place in the Pac-8 behind national kingpin UCLA with a 9–5 mark. In his junior year, he averaged 16.3 points per game in helping USC to a 24–2 overall record and a 12–2 mark in the Pac-8, good enough for second place, again behind UCLA. The Trojans were in the Associated Press Top 10 all season long, ending the season as the fifth-ranked team in the country. Their only two losses came to the Bruins. In his senior season, Westphal netted team highs of 20.3 points and 5.1 assists per game, and also averaged 5.3 rebounds per contest. The Trojans were the AP preseason number three team in the nation, but due to a left knee injury Westphal suffered about halfway through the schedule, causing him to miss the second half of the season, and other injuries, they fell to 16–10 overall and 9–5 in the conference.

As for a career in the NBA, Westphal realized in high school that he had a legitimate chance to get drafted. "I'd play summer indoor pickup games in high school and college at various places with some of the pros back then, and I did okay," he said. "I played some of those games with Wilt Chamberlain and Wille McCarter, guys like that. Those guys helped me a lot."

It was a no-brainer for the 6-foot-4, 195-pound Westphal when he was selected by the Boston Celtics in the first round of the 1972 NBA Draft and when he was drafted by the American Basketball Association's Denver Rockets that same year. "I was going to stay with Boston no matter what," he said. "That was an easy decision. It was a dream come true to get drafted by the Celtics."

Westphal's leg was in a cast when the Celtics drafted him. "Red [Auerbach] tried to use that against me a little bit," he said. "They took a chance that I'd recover, and it was probably a good break for me in a lot of ways because I got to get drafted by a great team. It worked out well for me. I appreciated the Celtics while I was growing up. I didn't root for anybody as much as I just really liked the game and appreciated the Celtics and the Lakers primarily."

There were several Celtics who took Westphal under their wings during his rookie season of 1972–73. "I think that, between Satch Sanders, Paul Silas, Don Nelson, and John Havlicek ... those guys in particular were really astute and very helpful in every way they could be," he recalled. "Red was also fantastic to me, just kind of pulling me aside every day to tell me things that he noticed and tell a story or two to let me know how they did things."

Westphal came off the bench for Boston in his first three seasons through 1974–75. "I wanted to play more," he said, "but I didn't think I was getting an unfair deal because I played behind Jo Jo White and Don Chaney, and they played 82 games every year and never got hurt. Those guys were ahead of me in the pecking order, they were great players, and the team was winning. What could I say?"

Westphal was traded to Phoenix and was the main man in the "Valley of the Sun" for five seasons through 1979–80. His best seasons were 1977–78 and 1978–79. In the former, he averaged both a team-leading 25.2 points and 5.5 assists per game. In the latter, he helped the Suns advance to the Western Conference finals, where they lost in heartbreaking fashion to Seattle.

Speaking of Seattle, that is where Westphal got traded on June 4, 1980, in exchange for Dennis Johnson. "After nine games with the Sonics, I developed a stress fracture in my right foot, and they didn't really know much about those," he said. "It doesn't show up on X-rays until they start healing, so they can't really diagnose what's wrong with you. I tried to play off and on. Basically, the stress fracture turned into a broken foot. I had two surgeries on the foot."

Westphal played in only 36 games for the SuperSonics in 1980-81, his lone season in Seattle, but he was still voted to his fifth straight All-Star game. He spent two seasons with New York before closing out his career back in Phoenix in 1983–84. That season, the Suns finished just 41–41, but like the 1975–76 Suns, became a Cinderella story and advanced all the way to the Western Conference finals, where they lost in six games to the Lakers.

Westphal, a member of the Naismith Memorial Basketball Hall of Fame and the College Basketball Hall of Fame, looks back on his playing career with great joy. "My rookie year," he said, "I just hoped to be able to play in the NBA, to play in the best league in the world, and see where it went. It was a dream come true to be able to have all the experiences I got in the NBA."

He began his coaching career in 1985–86 as head coach for Southwestern Conservative Baptist Bible College (now Arizona Christian University) in Glendale, Arizona. He spent the next two seasons as the head coach for Grand Canyon University in Phoenix. He began his NBA coaching career in 1988–89 as an assistant for Phoenix. He worked his way up to head coach of the Suns, a position he held until 1995–96. He also was the head coach for Seattle and Sacramento. He was an assistant coach for Dallas and Brooklyn.

Fully retired since 2016, Westphal and his wife, Cindy, live in Scottsdale, Arizona, and have two grown children, a son and daughter. He enjoys spending time with Cindy and their grandchildren. He likes to read, travel, and play golf, too. He is also on the board at Arizona Christian.

Westphal will never forget both times he led the Suns to the NBA Finals—as a player in 1976 and as the head coach in 1993. "Both seasons were as good as any season can be without winning the title," he said. "To be in Phoenix and to see how the city and the state of Arizona got behind those teams … I've never seen anything like it. Those two seasons were as special as a season can be. You look at the year Portland won the title in 1977 and how that city got behind the Trail Blazers that season, and there were some years in Boston where everything just went their way and the city was going crazy, and when the Knicks were great and New York went crazy for them … it was like that in Phoenix those two years.

"They're very, very special years."

Gar Heard

Gar Heard may be known by many NBA fans as the guy who hit the miracle jump shot that forced a third overtime during Game 5 of the 1976 finals. Heard, however, was not just some one-hit wonder. He had a fine career as a power forward for five teams from 1970–71 to 1980–81. He was a third-round draft pick of Seattle in 1970 out of the University of Oklahoma. He also played for Chicago, Buffalo, Phoenix, and San Diego.

He averaged double figures in points four times, with his high of 15.3 points per game coming in 1973–74 as a member of the Braves. He came close one other time, netting 9.7 points per contest three years later with the Suns. The 6-foot-6, 219-pound Heard also averaged double figures in rebounds twice, with a best of 11.7 in 1973–74. He came close two other times, averaging 9.9 rebounds per game in 1974–75 with Buffalo and 9.6 boards per contest with Phoenix in 1976–77.

Heard was also drafted by the ABA's New Orleans team, which soon after relocated to Memphis, Tennessee. "It was an easy decision to go to the NBA. There was no doubt about it," he said. "That was always my goal—to play in the NBA."

Veteran Tom Meschery took him under his wing during in his rookie season with the SuperSonics. "He kind of protected me and taught me a little bit about the NBA," said Heard. "My first season, I didn't play that much, but by the end of my second season I was starting."

Heard was traded to Chicago on October 20, 1972. After a year with the Bulls, he was dealt to Buffalo on September 10, 1973. "We had fun in Buffalo," he said. "We had some young guys like myself, Bob McAdoo, Randy Smith, and Ernie DiGregorio. We got the ball up and down the floor and scored a lot of points. [Head coach] Jack Ramsay kind of let us go. McAdoo was an amazing scorer. We took both Washington [seven games] and Boston [six games] to the limit in the playoffs but couldn't get over the top.

"I had a good run in Phoenix. We had a couple very good years. I had back problems toward the end of my career. I tried to play one more season in Europe, but my body just wouldn't let me do it, so I thought it was time to give it up."

Heard was born in Hogansville, Georgia, on May 3, 1948. "I was seven or eight years old when I got interested in sports," he said. "We always played basketball year-round in my neighborhood. We also played baseball in the backyard. I started playing organized basketball in the sixth grade."

At Ethel Knight High School in LaGrange, Georgia, Heard played football and basketball and was on the track and field team. He was a wide receiver in football and a high jumper in track. "I was always one of the better basketball players on the team," he said. "I started off playing center. My favorite sport was basketball because it was played inside, and I didn't like cold weather. As a freshman, I played a lot on the varsity team. By my sophomore season, I was starting and was probably one of the best players on the team. I was the leading scorer my last three years. We were pretty good my junior and senior years. We played only against black schools. My senior year, we lost only two games and got to the black schools state quarterfinals. I was the leading rebounder my last two years."

Heard began getting recruited by colleges his junior year. "A lot of the black schools came after me," he said. "A lot of the major colleges started coming after me my senior year. At that time, not many colleges in the South were recruiting black players. Besides Oklahoma, some of the schools I got letters from were Southern Illinois and I think Indiana, quite a few schools. Oklahoma and Southern Illinois were the two I whittled it down to. Oklahoma had some really good players, and I liked the coach, Bob Stevens, and the style of ball that he played. We were a running offense in high school, and Oklahoma was too. I chose Oklahoma and got a full ride. I played for the freshman team, but unfortunately, I never got to play for Stevens because he was fired before my sophomore year. He was replaced by John MacLeod, who was the head coach of the freshman team when I was on it. We probably had the best freshman team in Oklahoma history. I thought we were almost as good as our varsity team. I think we may have even beaten them once or twice. I played forward. And I started on the varsity team my last three years."

Heard, who majored in special education, had knee surgery at the end of his sophomore season and had an injury-plagued junior year. He was the Sooners' leading scorer (21.8 points per game) and rebounder (12.5 rebounds per game) his senior year in 1969-70 in helping his team to a 19–9 record. It was the program's first winning season in 10 years and its best season since 1946–47.

After retiring as a player, Heard sold real estate in Arizona for two or three years. He opened an arcade there, too, and ran that for a few years. He then got into coaching, getting his start as an assistant for Dallas under MacLeod. He was an assistant for five other teams and had short stints as a head coach with the Mavericks in 1992–93 and the Wizards in 1999–2000.

After retiring in 2005, Heard has enjoyed playing golf and hosting basketball camps in Hogansville once a year. He also likes spending time with his four grown children and three grandchildren. He lives in Paradise Valley, Arizona.

"I wish I could've been an NBA head coach for a longer time because I thought that I had a lot to offer," he said, "but things just didn't work out."

Things *did* work out, however, when it came to his playing career.

Alvan Adams

In seventh grade, Alvan Adams went out for his school's football team. "I went out for football because I lived in Oklahoma, and Oklahoma is football country," he said. "On the first day, we did a bunch of laying-in-the-grass calisthenics, and we had to line up across from somebody, get down in a stance and take two steps forward, pick the guy up, and run four steps. After practice, the coach pulled me aside and goes, 'Alvan, anybody who comes out for football in junior high makes the team, so if you want to play football, you can, but I really think you have a future in basketball.' And I said, 'Thank you very much, goodbye.' And that was my one day of football."

Basketball would eventually become Adams's sport of choice. Born in Lawrence, Kansas, on July 19, 1954, he was about a month old when his family moved to Oklahoma. Growing up in Oklahoma City, he started playing baseball around first grade. "I remember liking baseball a lot," he said. "Mickey Mantle was from Oklahoma, so everybody loved Mickey Mantle and the Yankees. I played third base because I was always a big kid, and I was the first guy who could throw the ball all the way from third base to first base. I was able to hit the ball really far. But then my last year I played, in sixth grade, the whole season I didn't get one hit, but I did get hit in the head and got to go to first base. That was the highlight of that season. A few years ago, I was talking to Bob Shirley, who played Major League Baseball for many years. He was a teammate of mine. Steve Largent, a future NFL Hall of Fame wide receiver, was his catcher. We were all in the same class. Bob reminded me, 'I was the one who hit you with the pitch!' I go, 'I don't remember it was you. I just remember getting hit in the head and getting to go to first base one time that whole season.'"

Adams's sixth-grade year was his last playing baseball. "I got to junior high in seventh grade," he said, "and they looked at all of us and lined us up and said, 'Well, you look like a good athlete, you're gonna play football,' 'Well, you're pretty tall, why don't you play basketball?' That's the way I remember it. So I go, 'Basketball? Okay.' And I took to it, really liked it, and I stopped playing baseball and started playing basketball."

In seventh grade, Adams was already 6-foot-1. He was 6-foot-3 by the eighth grade and 6-foot-5 by the ninth grade. "I never played anything but center all the way through high school," he said. "Our ninth-grade coach taught us a lot of the basics. I learned quickly and played a lot. I also played a lot of backyard basketball in my neighborhood. One of my friends had an eight-foot goal. One had a nine-foot goal and one had a 10-foot goal. I remember my progression. I'd shoot around a little bit at the eight-foot goal. Pretty soon, I could dunk there. Pretty soon, I could dunk at the nine-foot goal. And eventually I could dunk at the 10-foot goal. We had guys who were better athletes than me in junior high, but I was always the best tall player and developed pretty quickly."

Adams, who was 6-foot-9 by his junior year, started on the varsity team at Putnam City High School in nearby Warr Acres from his sophomore season through his senior year. "We had a pretty good team each year," he said. "We got close my first two years and then won the state championship my senior year."

Adams was recruited by many colleges. "I took about 15 official visits, which was way too many because it's just way too much input," he said. "Back then, you didn't have the resources to research schools like there is today. I visited from Duke to Oregon, from Notre Dame to Rice. My finalists were Kansas, Vanderbilt, and Oklahoma. And then UCLA called late. I hadn't made a decision by the time school was out my senior year. So I went out and visited Utah, Oregon, Cal Berkeley, Long Beach State, and UCLA. I met John Wooden, and they made me an offer, but in the end I decided, for different reasons, on Oklahoma [he received a full scholarship]. It was kind of important for me to go to a good football school. On my visit to Oklahoma, I watched the "Game of the Century," the great 1971 Nebraska-Oklahoma game in which Johnny Rodgers beat us. But, in the end, it really boiled down to the people—the head coach, John MacLeod, and the other four incoming freshmen. We were five of the six best Oklahoma senior basketball players that year in a really good recruiting class.

"I was disappointed that MacLeod left to go to Phoenix after my sophomore year because he was one of the main reasons I went to Oklahoma. But I wasn't disappointed long. I had my career in front of me in college, and I really wasn't thinking about professional basketball at that point. My first year, 1972–73, was the first year in Division I that freshmen were allowed to play varsity. I played varsity all three years I was there. I left after my junior year but went back later to earn my degree in 1998 in letters, which is history, literature, philosophy, and ancient and modern foreign language."

Late in his freshman year, after the season was over, Adams returned to his dorm, and there were two men standing outside his door. "I said, 'Hello,'" he recalled. "They said, 'We're here because we drafted you.' I said, 'I thought I was too tall for the military.' I don't remember for sure if I really said that. They said, 'We're with the Utah Stars. We, the ABA, just did a special underclassmen dispersal draft, and we chose you.' I talked to them a little bit and said, 'Well, I'm not leaving college. I'm having a blast here. I'm getting an education, I've got a girlfriend, we've got a good basketball team. Professional basketball?' Then I started thinking, 'Basketball as a job?' I'd never thought of it that way because we didn't grow up watching professional basketball. We were watching college football back then."

After his sophomore year, both MacLeod and Jerry Colangelo contacted Adams. "They said, 'We'd be interested in drafting you if you want to come out,'" he recalled. "And I said, 'Well, I'm getting an education and we've got a good team coming back. I want to stay in college.' Then, after my junior year, the Suns came back again and said to me, 'We've got the fourth pick in the draft. We're really interested in you.' I didn't see that we had a good team coming back, a contending team. My girlfriend and I were going to get married between our junior and senior years. I said to her, 'Hey, let's go play basketball in Phoenix.' Never been there, sounds fun. How often does a person get a chance to break into the professional ranks—the best basketball league in the world—with a coach who knows him?"

Adams hung up some impressive numbers in his three seasons playing for Oklahoma. He led the Sooners by far each season in points per game and rebounds per game. He was always at least 20/10 in points and rebounds per game. His best year was his junior year when he averaged 26.6 points and 13.3 rebounds per contest. Oklahoma finished 18–8 in each of his first two seasons. A first-round selection by Phoenix in the 1975 NBA Draft, the 6-foot-9, 210-pound Adams played with the Suns from 1975–76 through 1987–88. He was an All-Star his rookie season. He was very consistent throughout his career, averaging 14.1 points, seven rebounds, and 4.1 assists per game.

Not long after his final season as a player, Adams rejoined the Suns in a front-office capacity, on the facility management side for the Suns' brand-new America West Arena (now Talking Stick Resort Arena). He has held his current position of vice president, facility management for more than 20 years.

Adams lives in Phoenix with his wife, Sara. They have two grown children and four grandchildren. His hobbies are hiking and spending time with his family.

Curtis Perry

Curtis Perry's athletic heroes while he was growing up were Bill Russell, Arthur Ashe, Jim Brown, and Lew Alcindor (now Kareem Abdul-Jabbar). "Those people were more into social activism, the ability to have a platform to voice your opinion and work for change," he said. "In college at Southwest Missouri State University [now Missouri State University], we established a black student union. I gave the eulogy there for Martin Luther King Jr. when he was assassinated."

Not only was Perry an advocate of social activism, he was a pretty good basketball player, too. Born on September 13, 1948, in Kinston, North Carolina, he was three or four years old when his family moved to Washington, DC, where he grew up. "On the street where we lived, there were quite a few boys the same age as me. And everybody had a brother," he said. "We played all the sports— basketball, baseball, football. Sometimes we'd play one side of the street against the other. We'd play football in the snow on Thanksgiving. We had our own Turkey Bowl. We'd race each other up and down the street."

Perry picked up basketball when he had a couple of growth spurts. "I wasn't much of a player, but I could run and I could jump," he said. "I had no offensive game, but I got all the rebounds and blocked the other teams' shots. By the time I entered Western High School my sophomore year, I was 6-foot-5. The coach saw me walking down the hall one day between classes, and he asked me, 'Don't you want to play basketball?' And I said, 'Yeah, sure.' So I went out for the team. I thought everybody out there was much more skilled athletically than I was, so I went out for the junior varsity team. I needed to learn more and get some experience. I thought, with some hard work, I could get much better at the game. I played center and forward on the junior varsity team."

Perry had a friend who lived across the street from him who had a car. "We went to the playgrounds, and we played all summer after my sophomore year. And I got better at it," he said. "My junior and senior years, even though I still didn't have an offensive game, I started on the varsity team at forward."

At Southwest Missouri State, a Division II school, Perry started at power forward after four games on the varsity team his freshman year. "We lost by one point to Southern Illinois, which had Walt Frazier and Dick Garrett in the backcourt," he said. "At that time in Division II, freshmen couldn't play in national tournaments."

The following summer, in 1967, Perry went home and played on the playgrounds. He realized he needed to become more of an offensive threat. "By the time my sophomore season arrived, my offensive game was much better," he said. "I had a couple of teammates work with me on my shot, having a more consistent jump shot from 15 feet. We lost to Evansville [Indiana] in the regionals. My junior year, we went to the national championship game but lost to Kentucky Wesleyan. My senior year, we got beat in the regionals by South Dakota State."

Perry's offensive game had finally turned the corner. He averaged 24 points and 17 rebounds per game his senior season. He was the Bears' leading scorer his last two years and the leading rebounder his last three years. He didn't think about playing in the NBA until he started getting some feelers his senior year. He was drafted by San Diego in the third round in the NBA draft and by Virginia of the ABA in 1970. "Al Bianchi, my future assistant coach with the Suns, was the head coach of Virginia at the time," he said. "I chose San Diego because Pete Newell was the general manager of the Rockets, and he and his wife Florence were just aces to me as far as encouraging me to get better. I didn't play much at center, but Pete was in my corner, he kept encouraging me. My rookie year, John Trapp was the one who mentored me, told me where to eat in different cities, how to prepare for training camp, things like that. He was a good influence on me. When we played the Lakers, Wilt Chamberlain came over to the locker room to talk to me and was also a good influence on me."

On December 9, 1971, after the Rockets had relocated to Houston, the 6-foot-7, 220-pound Perry was traded to Milwaukee. He started at power forward and center for some very talented Bucks teams through 1973–74, including a memorable seven-game NBA Finals loss to Boston in his last season there. He was chosen by the New Orleans Jazz in the 1974 expansion draft but was traded to Phoenix before the start of the 1974–75 season. Perry hung up some pretty impressive numbers, including double figures in points per game his first three seasons as a Sun. His best season ever was his first in Phoenix when he averaged 13.4 points and 11.9 rebounds per game. He broke his back and missed the second half of the 1976–77 season. "I played hurt the first half of the '77–'78 season but just couldn't go anymore. I came back too early and it cost me my career," he said. "I tried to rehab in the summer of '78, but I failed the Suns physical, so I retired. It was very tough on me because I thought I was coming into my own as a player. It was like a really, really big kick in the stomach." He still has back problems to this day.

After retiring, Perry spent some time as a member of the Suns' speakers bureau talking about, among other things, the state of basketball, staying in school, and hard work. He taught school for a while and coached high school and junior high school basketball. He left Phoenix in 1999 to return to Washington, DC, to care for his ailing father. He taught school there until retiring in 2010 to care for his mother, who was ill. Perry, who enjoys playing chess, lives in DC and has two grown children, a son and a daughter. The son, Byron Houston, played for three NBA teams in the 1990s.

Keith Erickson

Keith Erickson had a solid 12-year career in the NBA playing for four teams mainly as a small forward. He averaged 9.5 points and 4.5 rebounds per game throughout his career. In the 1976 playoffs for Phoenix, however, Erickson came through big time in a handful of games in helping the Suns advance to the NBA Finals. He scored 31 points in a 130–114 victory over Seattle in Game 4 of the Western Conference semifinals and 24 points in the next game. In the Suns' 133–129 double-overtime win over heavily favored Golden State in Game 4 of the conference finals, he poured in 28 points. He scored 24 points in their 105–104 triumph over the Warriors in Game 6.

Erickson's long road to the NBA began when he was born in San Francisco on April 19, 1944. He was nine years old when his family moved south to El Segundo, California. "My father was an outstanding tennis player, so he had me out on the tennis courts when I was three or four years old," he said. "The racket was probably a little taller than I was. El Segundo was a tiny town, and the only two people there who played tennis at all were my father and me. I didn't like continuing to play with my dad when every one of my friends was out playing other sports. I wanted to play with them, so I quit tennis in eighth or ninth grade. I played baseball, basketball, and volleyball for my school teams. I started playing tennis again when I was out of college and played in the preliminaries in the open division of the Los Angeles Open."

Erickson started playing basketball competitively in ninth grade at El Segundo High School. He played forward on the freshman team, the sophomore team, the junior team, and the varsity team his senior year. "My senior year, I was probably the third- or fourth-best player on the team. I had no scholarship offers to play in college," he said. "I went to El Camino College, a community college in nearby Gardenia for a year, which was considered my freshman year. I played basketball and baseball there. We had a pretty good basketball team. I started at forward and center but was not the best player on the team. My coach there, George Stanich, had played for Coach [John] Wooden at UCLA. Stanich put in a good word for me to UCLA assistant coach Jerry Norman, who was Stanich's teammate at UCLA under Wooden. Stanich recommended me as someone who was young and had potential and maybe in the long run someone who might be able to play a little bit at UCLA. UCLA was the only school that offered me a scholarship. I got a half scholarship for basketball and a half scholarship for baseball."

UCLA had not won any championships before, so Wooden did not have the reputation he soon would have. "My sophomore year we qualified for the NCAA tournament, and my junior and senior years we won the national championship," said Erickson, who started at forward for the Bruins his last two years and averaged 12.9 points and 8.8 rebounds per game his senior season. "We had the best pair of guards ever to play college basketball—Walt Hazzard and Gail Goodrich. Hazzard was phenomenal. It was pretty unreal being on those teams. I wasn't an offensive player, so I rarely scored a lot of points. One of the things that Wooden taught over and over again was that it was the team, not individuals, that was important. I was just part of the team and was a defensive player and did my job defensively. I was happy to be there. Unfortunately, most of us playing for Wooden at the time were too young and immature to appreciate how great he was."

Not being a scorer or a well-known player, the 6-foot-5, 195-pound Erickson had no idea whether he was going to have an opportunity to try out for NBA teams. He wound up being a third-round pick by the San Francisco Warriors in the 1965 NBA Draft, the same draft in which the Warriors selected future Hall of Famer Rick Barry. "But I was the fourth player chosen by them, and there were only nine teams in the NBA at that time. So I wasn't going to go buy a house because there was no guarantee that I'd make the team."

Erickson ended up making the team and came off the bench. He was chosen by Chicago in the 1966 expansion draft. He started periodically for the Bulls in his second season there in 1967–68. He was traded to Los Angeles on September 23, 1968, and spent five glorious seasons with the Lakers, including winning the 1971–72 NBA title. Unfortunately, he was out due to surgery on both knees and missed playing in that finals series. "I played with Wilt Chamberlain, Elgin Baylor, and Jerry West," he said. "Those were some exciting times. Just to play alongside them and help them win games was tremendous. Wilt was the most dominant player ever,

Jerry was the most clutch shooter, and Elgin has been overlooked for years. He was one of the greatest players to ever play in the league."

Three weeks into the 1973–74 season, Erickson was traded to Phoenix. "I was just happy to still be playing," he said. "It was a good opportunity. It was a young franchise. Jerry Colangelo was running the team at that time. It was really fun to be there. Everybody was excited about the team. That '75–'76 season when we went to the finals was a great time because, as opposed to my time with the Lakers with three of the greatest players ever, in Phoenix we were more of a team. Paul Westphal and Alvan Adams were the two main players, but it was a chance for everybody to be part of a team. Not to take anything away from the Lakers experience, which was the greatest, but it was different with the Suns. It was more a team situation in Phoenix with everybody contributing different nights and different ways."

An arthritic hip caused Erickson to retire after the 1976–77 season. He was a color commentator for NBA games on CBS for two seasons and for Lakers and Clippers games on television and radio after that. He said that working alongside the great Chick Hearn on Lakers games was something he will never forget. "It was fantastic," he said. "He was one of the best basketball broadcasters ever. It was just a thrill to work with him. He was a real pro, he was prepared every night, and he had a great sense of humor. It was phenomenal."

Erickson then worked in sales for a friend's corrugated box business for a few years before returning to the color commentator's role for locally televised Suns games for seven years. Around 2000, he began working with two of his sons, including marketing in the insurance brokerage business. He is also a consultant with a couple other businesses in Los Angeles. Erickson lives with his wife, Adrienne, in Santa Monica, California. They have five grown children. Erickson's hobby is studying the Bible.

According to Erickson, his NBA career was very enjoyable, especially his time in Los Angeles. "To be able to play for the John Wooden-led UCLA basketball program was more than anything I could've asked for," he said. "Then to be able to play for the Los Angeles Lakers, one of the greatest franchises ever, alongside some of the greatest players of all time was just a great thrill."

John Shumate

They were laughing at John Shumate.

Shumate was trying out for the junior varsity basketball team as a freshman for Thomas Jefferson High School, an all-boys school in Elizabeth, New Jersey. "I was taller than most guys my age, and the guys who were the athletes in the neighborhood all had begged me to try out for the team, and I did," he said. "The tryouts were at Battin High School, the all-girls school. I didn't tell my parents that I was going because they were very strict, so I sneaked to go to the tryouts. It was the first time I ever touched a basketball, much less participated in any kind of an organized sports environment.

"The guys said, 'We need a center, we need a tall guy, we need you, you'll make the team.' I didn't even know how to bounce a ball; I didn't know how to shoot a ball. I got laughed out of the gym. And I was completely embarrassed and humiliated. The girls were trying out for cheerleading practice on one part of the court, and we were on the other part of the court. So the girls noticed how bad I was, and they were all laughing at me, too."

Little did Shumate know that eventually he would become a very good player in the NBA.

Born on April 6, 1952, in Greenville, South Carolina, Shumate's family moved to Newark, New Jersey, when he was two years old. After several years, it was on to Elizabeth. "That's where I really grew up," Shumate said. "I have five sisters. I was the only boy, so my parents were really strict with me. Most parents are stricter with girls than boys, but I had to abide by the same rules as my sisters. My father was a Pentecostal minister, so we were in church a lot. I wasn't allowed to really venture away far from home like a lot of guys, so the main sport that I played growing up was double-dutch hopscotch. We grew up in the projects, so I had to stay around with my sisters close to home because of the environment with drugs, crime, and so on. When I got a little older, I had a part-time job working in a barbershop as a shoeshine boy. Other than school, that was the only place my parents allowed me to go. Life was pretty boring to me because I couldn't go and do things that the other guys did."

On that day he got laughed at, Shumate snuck out of the gym and ran home crying because he was so humiliated. "The coach who was at the tryouts came to my house a couple hours later," he said. "I saw him, and I took off running. He grabbed me by the back of my pants and said, 'Hold it! Hold it!' I started crying and said, 'I was horrible, everybody was laughing at me. I was an embarrassment.' He said, 'I want to ask you one question, and then I'll let you go if you want to go.' And I stopped crying and said, 'Yeah, what?' And he said, 'Where did you get the footwork that you had?' And I'm trying to figure out, 'What do you mean, footwork?' I looked down. And he started laughing and said, 'Nobody had the great footwork that you had. Your lateral foot speed, agility, and quickness were superior. We, the coaching staff, are trying to figure out where you learned to have the footwork that you have.' And I'm scratching my head and I'm like, 'Oh, I don't kno-o-o-ow.' And he said, 'Well, tell me what some of the things are that you've done in your life.' I said, 'Hopscotch, double dutch, single dutch with my sisters.' And he started laughing, and I said, 'See? You're laughing at me.' And he said, 'No, no, that's it. That's where you got the tremendous footwork that you have. Listen, you have the hardest part already conquered. I can teach you the skills of basketball. I'll teach you basketball if you try out and make the commitment to the team. But you can't miss any practices."

Shumate then had an excitement in his spirit because he had never experienced anything like that where someone wanted him to do something athletically. "Summer was approaching, and before the coach left, he said, 'During the summer I'm going to have a group of guys every Saturday and Sunday. We're going to practice and get prepared for summer league play. The only commitment you have to make is that you have to work hard and not miss a practice without my say-so.' I said, 'Okay, no problem.' So when he walked away, I said, 'Oh heck!' I'd forgotten that because my dad was a preacher, I was in church on Saturdays and Sundays for Bible school and all of that stuff. And we had a revival coming up, which was going to be seven days a week. So, for the first time in my life, I rebelled and did something behind my mom and dad's back. I snuck out of the house that first Sunday, threw my clothes out the front window, and I got my clothes and I ran to the workout. It was so much fun, and I was learning really quick."

After the first workout, Shumate was walking home and, all of a sudden, he had a feeling of fear. "I said to myself, 'Oh my god, I didn't go to church, and mom and dad will be home,'" he remembered. "It was known throughout the neighborhood that, whatever I did, no matter how severe it was or wasn't, if it was something my dad didn't like that I did, he was coming after me whether it was out in the street or on the playground. Wherever he saw me, I'd get it right there. So whenever parents in the neighborhood saw me venturing away from home, they'd always say, 'You better get home. You know your dad's going to be there, and he'll tear you up.' And my heart would start beating fast and I'd run home. So after I got home from practice, I'm shaking like a leaf. This was the summer before my sophomore year, so I'm a little older, but I still had fear of my dad. That day, my mom and dad came home and he never asked me, 'Why weren't you in church? Why did you miss church?' He just came home and it was another day. Nothing ever happened. Later in the summer, he didn't know I'd been playing all summer because he was working all day. My mom worked as a nurse's aide at night, so she slept during the day, so she didn't know about my playing either. So whenever they had practice, I was there. And then I started going to the playground with the guys to play pickup ball with the older guys. And I was just improving by leaps and bounds. When my family was out one night, one of my sisters, about nine years old, yelled, 'There's Johnny playing basketball!' So my mom and dad stopped the car. They saw me dunk the ball. I was always intimidated by my dad, but I wasn't afraid. I hit a shot to win the game. He walked up to me after the game and said, 'You're pretty good.'"

Shumate wound up making the junior varsity team as a sophomore. By that time, he was 6-foot-5. "The coach of the JV team was our summer league coach," he said. "I started at center all the way through my senior year. I made the varsity team as a junior. By then, I was a legitimate player. I was projected to be an All-American player the next year. I was All-State as a senior in 1969–70. Everybody started telling me how good I was, and I started thinking, *Wow! Maybe one day I can make it to the NBA.*

Shumate was recruited pretty much by every major school in the country. "Initially, I wanted to go to UCLA," he said. "There was a big brawl at one of our games my senior year. One of my teammates got caught up into a fight, and so we were all protecting my teammate, and we're all fighting. The crowd came onto the floor, and I was in the middle of it. And [future Louisville head coach] Denny Crum, a UCLA assistant coach at the time, was there at the game. The word that I got was that Crum told John Wooden, UCLA's living legend of a head coach at the time, that I was a bad guy, that he didn't think he'd want to recruit me." Wooden listened to his assistant.

Notre Dame ended up winning the John Shumate sweepstakes. Shumate received a full scholarship. After playing forward and center on the Fighting Irish's freshman team, positions he would continue playing on the varsity squad, Shumate had an illness that caused him to miss his entire sophomore season. "The doctors said I'd never play basketball again," he said.

Not only did Shumate prove the doctors wrong, he led Notre Dame in scoring and rebounding his junior and senior seasons. As a junior, he averaged 21 points and 12.2 rebounds per game. "By that time," he said, "I knew for sure I could make it to the pros because, by then, I'd played against all of the top players and was very dominant in every game that I played in."

As a senior, Shumate netted 24.2 points and 11 boards per contest in helping the Irish to a 26–3 record and a win in the NCAA tournament. That season, on January 19, 1974 at home, Notre Dame upset top-ranked UCLA, 71–70, breaking the Bruins' all-time best 88-game winning streak. "I had a big game," said Shumate. "It was probably the biggest thing that had ever happened to me. Such a huge game, both teams undefeated, every TV camera in the U.S. was there prior to the game and at our practice. It was packed with media—print media and electronic media. So it was a huge, huge deal. For me, it was the biggest moment of my career and of my life playing on national television like that.

"We played UCLA the following week at UCLA, and I had another big game even though we lost. Coach Wooden came into our locker room and said to me, 'I don't make many mistakes in this game, but one big mistake I made was not recruiting you. I want to congratulate you for representing this sport as an outstanding young man. You've represented yourself, your family, and Notre Dame with nothing but praise and high character. You've done very well for yourself, and I'm very proud of you.' And he hugged me. That made me feel good because I was really disappointed that they didn't recruit me. It was a proud moment for me."

After graduating in 1974 with a degree in sociology, the 6-foot-9, 235-pound Shumate was a first-round draft pick—the fourth overall selection—by Phoenix that year. "I was excited," he said. "To be a top-five pick and go from nowhere, being an unknown and never playing ball until high school, and now being the fourth player picked in the draft behind Bill Walton, Marvin Barnes, and Tom Burleson, it couldn't have been any better than that. It was quite an accomplishment."

Shumate sat out the 1974–75 season due to blood clots. "That was difficult for me," he said. "I didn't really have a chance to be the player that I thought I could be. My career was disrupted with illnesses that I had. Once I had the illness in the NBA, that was when teams started looking at me kind of sideways because I was kind of damaged goods by then."

After averaging 11.3 points per game in 43 games for the Suns in 1975–76, Shumate was traded to Buffalo on February 1, 1976. "The night I went to Buffalo after getting traded, I went to bed and woke up the next morning to a wind chill factor of 30 degrees below zero," he recalled. "They had so much snow that fell when I got there that it was more than 30 inches of snow that had fallen. There was so much snow, the national guard came in to push it to the sides of the roads. The next morning, I was going to go to practice with my teammate Kenny Charles, but there was so much snow that we couldn't find his car! After that experience, I decided that, after I retired, I'd make my home in Phoenix.

"By the time I was traded to Buffalo, it was going to be a sketchy road for me. If I got sick again, then I was going to be on my way out because teams would be leery of having me because of the potential for me to die from blood clots and also the years I couldn't play they still had to pay me for."

The Braves dealt Shumate to the Pistons on November 23, 1977. He missed the 1978–79 season due to the same illness he had his sophomore year in college. He played for three more teams—Houston, San Antonio, and Seattle—through his final season of 1980–81. Shumate averaged 12.3 points and 7.5 rebounds per game during his NBA career.

Shumate returned to Phoenix and worked in parks and recreation. He returned to the Suns and worked in community relations and scouting.

He is currently a Suns ambassador. He and his wife, Mary, live in Phoenix and have a grown son and grown daughter.

Dennis Awtrey

Baseball was Dennis Awtrey's favorite sport as a young boy. He played Little League from ages eight to twelve. Born in Hollywood, California, on February 22, 1948, Awtrey played baseball, basketball, and football in the street with the other neighborhood kids. Basketball soon overtook baseball as his sport of choice. His family moved to San Jose, California, when he was 10 years old. "I never played organized basketball until I got into junior high school," he said. "I was always tall, but I wasn't the tallest player on the team until I got to college. We always had somebody who was a little taller than me. I started high school [Blackford High] at 6-foot-1 or so and by my senior year I was 6-foot-9. I was always a center at all levels. It wasn't until my sophomore year that I became a starter on the varsity team. We enjoyed some success as a team in high school. I was the best player on the team my junior and senior years. I averaged almost 30 points per game both years."

Several colleges recruited Awtrey. He visited Duke, Washington, Santa Clara, and UCLA. "I met with John Wooden, UCLA's head coach," he said. "He had an aura about him. He was calm. You just had total respect for him. You had to look up to him.

"My high school coach was a Stanford graduate. He was always there to help me, but he never tried to push me one way or another. I knew Santa Clara University very well because I was in the area. I used to play there in the summers, pickup ball a couple nights a week. I got to know and like the coaches there a lot, and I respected them a lot. Duke had a really good program, and UCLA was obviously UCLA. UCLA was also recruiting a guy by the name of Steve Patterson. He was a little shorter than I was. When I went down for my visit to UCLA, they took me to a Lakers playoff game at the LA Sports Arena. I looked at the other end, and there was Steve and some USC guys. One of the UCLA guys told me they were not recruiting him anymore. And I didn't care if they were or not. I was confident in myself. And the next week Steve signed with UCLA.

And that caused a lack of trust. It made me worry. And Duke was on the other side of the country, so I decided to stay local and go to Santa Clara on a full ride."

"When you're 6-foot-9 in high school, banging isn't going to affect you because you're just so much bigger and stronger than everybody else. In college, our team was a very physical team, and that's the way I always believed you should play basketball. Not hitting anybody or holding or grabbing, but I didn't mind leaning on a guy. At the same time, he's free to lean on me. I didn't care. That was fair."

Awtrey was the starting center on the Broncos' freshman team which finished 21–1 in 1966–67. He was the starter on the varsity team his three remaining seasons. It was at the end of my sophomore year that I realized I had a chance to play in the NBA. My sophomore and junior years we were 22–4 and 27–2, respectively, but lost to UCLA in the NCAA tournament West Regional final. My senior year, we were 23–6 and lost to Utah State in a West Regional semifinal. We played well together. We were a good team. You wanted to play hard for Dick [Garibaldi], the head coach. You loved the guy." Awtrey led the team in scoring (21.3 points per game) his junior year and rebounding (high of 14.1 per game his senior year) all three seasons.

The 6-foot-10, 235-pound Awtrey was chosen by the Philadelphia 76ers in the third round of the 1970 NBA Draft. "I split the starting center duties my rookie year with Connie Dierking and Luke Jackson," he said. "Bill Bridges took me under his wing my second year there. He really taught me about setting picks, rebounding, and stuff like that. I was traded to Chicago very early in the '72–'73 season because Tom Boerwinkle blew out his knee. With Chicago, we had some real good teams. In '72–'73, we could've gone all the way. We lost to the Lakers in seven in the Western Conference semifinals. We had the lead in Game 7 with about a minute to go. I started most of that season. I was mainly a backup the next season.

"Those Chicago years are my best NBA memories. I really enjoyed playing for those teams. They were feisty teams. With Jerry Sloan and Norm Van Lier at the guards, there was no more intensity that you could have. And Chet Walker and Bob Love were great scorers. Dick Motta did a great job coaching those teams. Playing in Chicago Stadium was fabulous. It was really, really neat. It was a historic place; the crowds were great. There were times when we had 22,000 people in there, but they didn't tell people it was that many because the fire marshal didn't like it. Chicago is a great sports town."

After Awtrey was taken by New Orleans in the 1974 expansion draft, he wound up being traded to Phoenix. He was the Suns' starting center in 1974–75. When Alvan Adams was drafted the next year, Awtrey was relegated to backup status through 1977–78, his final season with the team. He closed out his NBA career with Boston, Seattle, the Bulls again, and Portland, including being a member of the league champion SuperSonics in 1978–79. He played in Europe for a while before retiring. "I lost my fire. There were injuries, too," he said. "Retiring was the best thing that ever happened to me. It was a blessing."

Awtrey returned to Phoenix and worked in real estate for Coldwell Banker as a coordinator for Ping golf clubs in the junior golf division and taught high school before taking some time off. Then, in 2011, he and his wife, Peggy, built a home on the Oregon coast and started a bed and breakfast. "I've really enjoyed it," said Awtrey, who has two grown children from a previous marriage. "It's the most fun I've had since I played ball. The bed and breakfast is in a little town called Manzanita, about 80 miles from Portland, a town of about 700 people. It's a spectacular house with a spectacular view of the Pacific Ocean. It's fun."

Awtrey, who is an avid reader and golfer, has no problem with the amount of money that today's athletes make. "If you're in pro sports," he said, "you're one of the luckiest people in the world to do what you're doing. Some people have a problem with the amount of money guys are making playing pro sports. I say, hey, as long as they're working hard and having fun, I don't care. Make as much money as you can. One time I woke up in the morning in Phoenix and saw that Shawn Marion had just signed a 13 and a half million-dollar a year contract. My best season, I made one percent of what he was making. One percent! He made more in one game than I made in an entire season! But he played hard. I say, look where I'm living. I have no complaints. It'd be nice to make that kind of money, but, hey, I'm happy."

Fred Saunders

When Fred Saunders was in the eighth and ninth grades, he played basketball for his junior high school. The games were played in the daytime, which was a good thing since his father was a minister and did not allow his son to play sports at night. But when the younger Saunders got to high school, those games were played in the evening. "My father realized how good I was, so he had to let me play," he said.

Born in Columbus, Ohio, on June 13, 1951, Saunders played basketball and baseball as a youngster and added football to his resume when he got to Mohawk High School. "I was a wideout, punter, and placekicker in football, a pitcher and first baseman in baseball, and a center in basketball," he said. "By the time I was a senior, I was 6-foot-7, and I was done growing. My senior year, we were the number one team in the state in Class AAA, the big schools. We should've won the state championship, but we lost one game—in the tournament to [Columbus] Walnut Ridge."

Saunders got a full ride to play basketball at the University of Southwest Louisiana (now the University of Louisiana at Lafayette), where he played forward and guard. "My goal was to be prepared to be a pro by the time I was a junior," he said. Saunders helped the Ragin' Cajuns to a 25–4 record his sophomore year and a 24–5 mark his junior year. Both seasons, they qualified for the NCAA tournament and won a game. Saunders transferred to Syracuse University his senior year, where his 9.8 points and 9.8 rebounds per game as a forward and guard helped the Orangemen (now the Orange) to a 19–7 record and a berth in the 1973–74 NCAA tourney.

Saunders also was a starter on a team that the United States put together in 1973. "We'd lost the [Olympic] gold medal to Russia in '72," he said. "We had to save face, so they put together this team in which Bob Cousy was the head coach. We played the Russians in a seven-game series in the United States at different sites across the country. We beat them six out of the seven games with guys like Ernie DiGregorio, Bill Walton, Swen Nater, and George Karl. Walton played in only two games, though, due to bad knees."

Selected by Phoenix in the second round of the 1974 NBA Draft, the 6-foot-7, 210-pound Saunders was certain he would make it in the NBA.

"I was ready to go," he said. "When I dunked on the Sixers' Clyde Lee my rookie year, I realized I belonged in the NBA."

Saunders was waived by the Suns on February 11, 1976, and signed with Boston during that year's NBA Finals. The Celtics traded him to New Orleans halfway through the 1977–78 season. The Jazz waived him a little more than a week before the start of the next season. He played in the Western League and the Continental Basketball League before retiring. He worked in Louisiana as a maintenance man for Sunoco in the oil fields for two-and-a-half years and then sold annuities for a year. He sold cars for about 30 years off and on, taught school for 20 years, and was the head basketball coach for Franklin Heights High School in the Columbus area before retiring for good in 2012. He and his wife, Rebecca, live in Columbus. He has a grown daughter from a previous marriage. He volunteers for the basketball team at Pickerington Central High School and is an Uber driver on the side.

John Wetzel

When John Wetzel was visiting the few colleges that recruited him for basketball, his trip to Virginia Military Institute made a lasting impression—but not a positive one. "Every day when the guys left the room to go to class, they had to roll up their mattresses and put everything away," he said. "I said to myself, 'There ain't no way I'm gonna do that! I can't do this every day!' I didn't have the desire to live like that."

Wetzel was also recruited by the University of Virginia and got a letter from the University of North Carolina, but he wound up going to Virginia Tech. "Virginia Tech just felt right," he said. "I had a real good rapport with the players and coaches. I felt really comfortable there, and my lifestyle fit perfectly there. The atmosphere was really good for me."

After playing forward on the freshman team that lost just one game in 1962–63, Wetzel continued at the same position on the varsity team his last three years. He averaged a team-leading 14.3 points per game and netted 6.7 rebounds per game his junior year. As a senior, he led the 19–5 Hokies with both 18.5 points per game and 8.8 rebounds per contest. "We came alive that season," he said.

Born in Waynesboro, Virginia, on October 22, 1944, Wetzel was in fifth or sixth grade when he gained an interest in sports and played backyard basketball. "I had two older brothers, and they'd, on occasion, take me with them to the high school basketball game," he said. "Going to watch the high school team play was really fascinating to me."

Wetzel did not play organized basketball until he attended Wilson Memorial High School in Fishersville, Virginia. He was also on the track and field team. After playing forward on the freshman team, he played the same position his last three years. "With maybe five games remaining in the season my sophomore year they moved me from the junior varsity team up to the varsity team," he said. "I got better and I started to grow. I was really thin and small when I started high school. At the start of my freshman year I was 5-foot-7 and 111 pounds. I was 5-10 at the end of my freshman year. By my senior year, I was 6-4. I was the best player on the team my last two years. I improved the most. I was really dedicated. I'd go out in the summer by myself and shoot balls. I wanted to go play ball as much as I could. Because of that, I continued to get better whereas the other guys didn't play much in the summer, so they didn't improve as much as I did. My senior year, the only game we lost was in the state championship game for smaller schools. We were 22–1."

Up to his junior year, Wetzel did not have any long-term goals. "I just wanted to be as good as I could and play as well as I could for our team," he said. "When I got a few letters and phone calls from colleges my senior year, that's when I thought, *Well, maybe you do have a chance to go on and play more.* Until that point, I'd never really entertained those kinds of thoughts because I didn't know that I was going to get better."

Wetzel was drafted by the Los Angeles Lakers in the eighth round in 1966 but did not start playing with them until the 1967–68 season because he broke his wrist during the '66 training camp. During that time, he went back to school as a graduate assistant. "Probably the guy who was most helpful to the younger players my rookie year was Jerry West," he said. "He'd give tips through practice. Right near the end of training camp, he broke his wrist. They put me in the starting lineup for the first 12 games until he got back." The Lakers advanced all the way to the NBA Finals, where they lost in six games to Boston.

ROGER GORDON

The 6-foot-5, 190-pound Wetzel, who came off the bench for the most part throughout his NBA career, was taken by Phoenix in the 1968 expansion draft, but he missed the next two seasons due to military obligations. He spent the 1970–71 and 1971–72 seasons with the Suns. "I figured out early in my career how it worked and how I fit in regarding my NBA career," he said. "I was a good teammate, and I played when I was called on. There were a lot of games where I played limited minutes or didn't play at all. And I sat there and cheered the team on and did the best I could in practice. When I got a chance, I went in and played hard. I was what you would call a journeyman NBA player. I saw young players who were stars in college come in the league and were sitting on the bench, and they couldn't accept it. They didn't know how to adapt. I figured out early that whatever the coach wants you to do, do it. If it means sit there, do it. I learned not to be a distraction, to be a positive. That was my attitude. I tried to play that way and conduct myself that way."

Wetzel was waived on October 9, 1972, and signed as a free agent with Atlanta midway through the 1972–73 season. He spent two and a half seasons with the Hawks before returning to Phoenix for his swan song in 1975–76. He retired the following summer. "I was 31, and I made up my mind that I'd played long enough," he said. "It was getting really hard to get in shape with training camp. I went back to Virginia Tech and got my degree in general science. It made it easy for me to transition because I wasn't in an NBA city looking at games, looking at box scores, and reading about the team every day. I just got completely away, and I had schoolwork to do. The assistant athletic director who recruited me in high school was still there. He asked me if I'd coach the women's team, so I coached the women's team in the first year it was a varsity sport. So I was busy with that and with school. After one season, I coached a minor league basketball team up in the Tri-Cities area in the state of Washington for a year. It was the equivalent to today's NBA G League.

"When I was a player, I'd given coaching a thought. When you sit on the bench and you don't play a lot, you really pay attention to what's going on, how the game evolves, and the backups. So I thought I'd have a chance to do that."

Wetzel got into NBA coaching in 1979–80 as an assistant with the Suns through 1986–87. He was their head coach in 1987–88, finishing

28–54. "It was hard," he said. "We weren't a particularly good team. Our team was fragmented because of some drug problems on the team the season before."

Wetzel went on to be an assistant coach for Portland, including two trips to the finals, New Jersey, Golden State, and Sacramento before retiring in 2004. He and his wife, Diane, have two grown sons. He and Diane spend half the year living in Marana, Arizona, and the other half of the year living in Makawao, Hawaii. "I play a little golf, my wife and I ride our bikes a couple times a week, and we hike a little bit when we're in Arizona," he said. "Now a big sport that we both participate in is outrigger canoe paddling in Maui. We compete in the age 70s division. We've gone to Australia and Egypt to compete."

13

THE GREEN AND WHITE

Dave Cowens

When Dave Cowens was on the Florida State University basketball team, he would emulate Boston Celtics great Bill Russell. "We used to play one-on-one before every practice, and I was Bill Russell because he was left-handed. And I liked the Celtics," he said on the *Legends with Leyden* show. "They were one of the only teams you really saw on TV back then."

Soon after the Celtics chose him in the first round of the 1970 NBA Draft, Cowens was at a basketball camp hosted by Red Auerbach. "Red and Tom Heinsohn were trying to figure out whether I was going to be a center, a forward … 'What should we do?'" he said. Bill Russell was there, too. "That's when Russell said, 'Look, don't tell this kid he can't do anything. Just let him go. He'll be fine.' That was kind of his recommendation."

"Big Red" proved Russell prophetic. From his first training camp on, he was like a bull in a china shop. Much shorter than most NBA centers, the 6-foot-9, 230-pound Cowens pounded opposing centers into oblivion. He was a very physical player. Not surprisingly, he led the NBA in fouls his rookie season of 1970–71. He also was voted co-Rookie of the Year with Portland's Geoff Petrie by averaging 17 points and 15 rebounds per game. Those numbers stayed right in the same vicinity throughout his NBA career. In a win over the Houston Rockets on March 20, 1973, Cowens scored 20 points and had a remarkable 32 rebounds plus nine assists. He was a key cog in Boston's NBA championship teams in 1974 and 1976.

As a testament to his all-around ability, he is one of only five players to lead his team in all five major statistical categories for a season—points, rebounds, assists, blocked shots, and steals. He accomplished the feat in 1977–78, averaging 18.6 points, 14 rebounds, 4.6 assists, .9 blocked shots, and 1.3 steals.

Injuries prompted Cowens to retire after the 1979–80 season. After sitting out two seasons, Cowens felt the itch to come back and give it another try. He spent the 1982–83 season with the Milwaukee Bucks and then retired from playing for good. An eight-time All-Star, he is a member of the Naismith Memorial Basketball Hall of Fame and the College Basketball Hall of Fame.

Born on October 25, 1948, in Newport, Kentucky, Cowens starred at Central Catholic High School. At Florida State, he led the Seminoles in scoring and rebounding his sophomore through senior years. In total, he averaged 19 points and a whopping 17.2 rebounds per game in leading his team to 19–8, 18–8, and 23–3 records. FSU qualified for its first-ever NCAA tournament his sophomore season of 1967–68.

Cowens served as the Celtics' player-coach for the final 68 games of the 1978–79 season, but he returned the next season as a player only. He coached in the Continental Basketball Association in the 1984–85 season. He returned to the NBA in 1994 with the San Antonio Spurs, where he was an assistant through 1996. He was the head coach of the Charlotte Hornets in the late 1990s and the Golden State Warriors from the start of the 2000–01 season until December 2001. He led the Hornets to a 51–31 record in 1997–98. He coached in the WNBA in 2005–06 and concluded his coaching career as an assistant for the Pistons from 2007 to 2009.

He believes the NBA game was much better in his days as a player than it is now. "Since they put the three-point line in, for me, as a big guy," he said on *Legends with Leyden*, "the degree of difficulty to sit there and shoot [the ball] from 23 feet with nobody guarding you is not as difficult as me shooting a hook shot over [Wilt] Chamberlain or [Kareem Abdul-] Jabbar or somebody like that. The game has changed really. It's [now] more important to get a 22-foot shot from the corner than it is to get a layup. [Now] you attack the basket for one purpose—to throw it to somebody out there to get that three-point shot. The game is so much different because everything's off the dribble. Before, it was pass the ball, make cuts, give it to a guy, he goes up and shoots. We didn't really like a lot of dribbling because there are more turnovers when you dribble a lot."

Cowens ran as a Republican for Massachusetts secretary of the commonwealth in 1989. However, because he did not register by the deadline, he was unable to appear on the primary ballot. He eventually dropped out of the race. He also hosted a children's basketball camp beginning in 1972.

As for his playing career with the Celtics, Cowens had a great time. "I hope the people that watched us saw that we really enjoyed ourselves as a group," he said on *Legends with Leyden*. "We were pretty good for a stretch of five or six years there. We had a chance to win a championship, and that's all you want. You never know if it's actually going to happen. There are no guarantees. I think we stimulated the Boston crowd about basketball a little bit."

Jo Jo White

When he was in high school at St. Louis McKinley, Jo Jo White tried out for the junior varsity basketball team.

He was cut.

"So what did I do? I went out for the varsity team and made it!" he said in his Naismith Memorial Basketball Hall of Fame acceptance speech. "Jodie Bailey, the head coach, was a great role model who taught self-discipline and fundamentals of the game."

Born on November 16, 1946, in St. Louis, White began playing basketball when he was six years old. It took a while for his parents to buy in to his love for the sport and the many hours he spent practicing at night. Mom and Dad finally went to watch their son play in a high school game.

Jo Jo put on a clinic. His parents were no longer skeptical. All was validated. But after the game, Mrs. White told Jo Jo that his socks were sort of at half-mast, something that became a trademark of his years later when he was playing for the Boston Celtics. Jo Jo brought that with him his whole life because it meant that his mother was paying attention to him on that court that night and that he had her support. "I was just proud to have my parents at one of my games. I'd been trying to get them to come," he said on the LATV show *Cityscope*. "Me being the youngest of seven and the way my parents raised us, wanting to know where the kids were all the time and to think that you might be doing something other than what you should be doing went against the grain of how we were raised. So to have my parents see me play for the first time helped them realize how excited I was to be able to play and master this game the way I had thus far in my career. It was just so great for me to have them there."

White had some 350 offers to play basketball in college. "My mother pretty much made the decision for me to go to the University of Kansas because she really fell in love with Ted Owens, the head coach," White said on *Cityscope*.

During his visit to Kansas before he signed to play there as a senior in high school, White got to see the great Gale Sayers play football against Oklahoma. "Just watching him play was … seeing an athlete maneuver as well as he did as a football player just took my breath away," said White on *Cityscope*. "I found myself *staring*. I played football as well, and [Sayers] wanted me to play football for the University of Kansas, but basketball was my love, so I dared not go that route."

Asked how he felt the first time he walked into Allen Fieldhouse for a game and saw Wilt Chamberlain's jersey hanging in the rafters, White said he was in awe. "I had never seen or been around players of that size and magnitude," he said on *Cityscope*. "I got a chance to meet Wilt for the very first time, and I was in awe just seeing him in person.

"They used to say that [Kansas] was a big man's school, so I had a determination to have a backcourt player do well there."

White did just that.

He helped revitalize the Jayhawks program, which had fallen into mediocrity after years of success, including three appearances in the NCAA championship game from 1951–52 to 1956–57, one of which they won, in 1952. With White, a guard, averaging 11.3 points and 7.6 rebounds per game as a freshman in 1965–66, Kansas finished 23–4 and almost advanced to the Final Four. In the Midwest Regional final, the Jayhawks played Texas Western (now Texas El Paso). During the first overtime, White connected on a 35-foot shot at the buzzer that would have won the game, but it was ruled that he was out of bounds. White and his teammates wound up losing a thriller, 81–80, in double overtime. The next season, the Jayhawks once again finished 23–4 and qualified for the NCAA tournament. As a junior, White led the Jayhawks in scoring with 15.3 points per game. His senior year, he tied for the team lead in scoring at 18.1 points per contest. "I always strived to be the best," he said in his Hall of Fame acceptance speech. "I also had two great mentors at the University of Kansas—Owens and the team's assistant coach, Sam Miranda."

The 6-foot-3, 190-pound White, a member of the United States's gold medal-winning Olympic team in 1968, was taken by Boston in the first round of the 1969 NBA Draft. He was a contributor at point guard right from the start, averaging 12.2 points per game in his rookie season of 1969–70. His best individual season with the Celtics was 1971–72 when he hung up 23.1 points, 5.6 rebounds, and 5.3 assists per contest. He led Boston to NBA titles in 1974 and 1976. In his Celtics career, he averaged 18.4 points, 4.3 rebounds, and 5.1 assists per game. "Being drafted by the Boston Celtics was one of the best things to ever happen to me," said White in his Hall of Fame acceptance speech. "Red Auerbach was tough and a blatantly honest guy who I love and have so much respect for. Our coach, Tommy Heinsohn, was demanding and tough, but always fair, and he was a winner. He always had my back. I had so many wonderful teammates over the years." White, a seven-time All-Star, was traded to Golden State on January 30, 1979. His swan song was spent with the Kansas City Kings in 1980–81. He passed away on January 16, 2018.

Charlie Scott

Charlie Scott pulled a Jackie Robinson nearly 20 years after Robinson became the first African American player in Major League Baseball for the Brooklyn Dodgers in 1947. In 1966, Scott became the first black scholarship athlete at the University of North Carolina. After starring on the Tar Heels' freshman team his first season, Scott was a starting guard his last three years. He helped lead the North Carolina program from mediocrity to heights it had not enjoyed since it won the NCAA title in 1957. Scott was an offensive machine, averaging 22.1 points per game in his three seasons on the varsity team. He also netted 7.1 rebounds per game. He averaged a career-best 27.1 points per contest his senior year. He led the Tar Heels to the national championship game his sophomore year and to the Final Four his junior year.

As great as he was on the court, though, it was his performance off it that was truly superb and an inspiration. "To see the South in the sixties is to see a society where I would never be thought of as a human being. I had no relationship with my teammates," he said on the *All Access with Carolina Basketball* television program. "My college experience was not a college experience because the things that made North Carolina North Carolina my teammates could not enjoy with me. I could not go to fraternities with them, I couldn't go to parties with them, we couldn't hang out together, we had nothing in common. I played basketball at North Carolina. They never interacted with a black person before on an intimate basis. It was new to them. I never interacted with a white person before. My first year, I made basketball my life. I would come to the gym by myself, I would work out by myself, I would play by myself. I worked on my skills because there was nothing really I could do on campus with anybody else because it would ostracize them."

Scott knew exactly what he was getting himself into when he came to North Carolina. "I knew I wasn't coming to a school where integration was a part of this society," he said on the show. "I knew that there were a lot of people who would dislike me. But it was the civil rights era, and responsibility was something that I really understood. Three years of playing basketball at North Carolina, I never felt happy about something. I always felt relieved that I was able to get through what I had to do. I never got an opportunity to really enjoy what I was doing. I scored 40 points in the [ACC] championship game against Duke and went back to the hotel that evening and just felt relief."

According to Scott, there were many people who were just waiting for him to take a misstep. "There was a lot of whites that were waiting for me to do something where they would say, 'See, I told you these blacks were going to mess up our university.' One of the things people never even knew, [head] Coach [Dean] Smith took away something for me because they used to play 'Dixie' [a song that was popular in the South in the nineteenth century] here at Carolina before the games. A lot of blacks wanted to know what I was going to do when they played 'Dixie'. What Coach Smith did was, the team would always go back into the locker room right after we finished warming up at the same time they would start playing 'Dixie'. So I never had to deal with 'Dixie' being played on my home court. What I couldn't do was be an outward leader because it would fracture the university system with those who were trying to get integration because my purpose of coming here was to integrate the school."

Scott was born on December 15, 1948, in New York City. He grew up primarily in Harlem and attended Stuyvesant High School in New York City his freshman year before transferring to Laurinburg Institute in Laurinburg, North Carolina, where he honed his skills on the basketball court. He was valedictorian of his senior class. During his college days at North Carolina, Scott was a member of the United States' gold medal-winning team at the 1968 Summer Olympics in Mexico City.

The 6-foot-5, 175-pound Scott was chosen by the Boston Celtics in the seventh round of the 1970 NBA Draft, but he had already signed a contract with the Virginia Squires of the ABA. As a guard (where he would play for his entire professional career), he was the ABA's Rookie of the Year in 1970–71, averaging a team-high 27.1 points per game. The next season, he hung up a league-high 34.6 points per contest in teaming with a rookie by the name of Julius Erving but decided to switch to the NBA late in the season and was traded by the Celtics to Phoenix. He continued to put up impressive offensive numbers in three-plus seasons with the Suns. He was traded back to Boston on May 23, 1975 and played a huge role on the Celtics' NBA title-winning team in 1975–76. He was dealt to the Lakers during the 1977–78 season and the following summer to the Nuggets, for whom he played his final two seasons before retiring. A five-time All-Star, Scott is a member of the Naismith Memorial Basketball Hall of Fame and the College Basketball Hall of Fame.

Scott was marketing director for the sports apparel company Champion for several years and was executive vice president of CTS, a telemarketing firm, before owning his own business. He and his wife, Trudy, have three grown children. Scott has a grown daughter from a previous marriage. His oldest son and one of his daughters followed in his footsteps and are graduates of North Carolina. Said Dad on *All Access with Carolina Basketball*, "I enjoyed vicariously through what I heard my kids say how much they loved it there and enjoyed the whole essence of what North Carolina is about."

John Havlicek

Before he joined the Boston Celtics in 1962, John Havlicek was known as more of a defensive player than an offensive player.

It didn't take long for that to change.

"I can recall a situation in a game where I was looking to make the pass and make a cut, and the defensive person wasn't even concerned or guarding me," Havlicek recalled in an NBA TV video. "And [head coach] Red [Auerbach] said, 'John, you can't let them insult you. You've got to shoot the ball when you have a chance.'"

Havlicek only needed to be told that one time.

"I think I've taken probably more shots than anyone in Celtics history," he said in the video. It wasn't long before the 6-foot-5, 203-pound Havlicek's points per game average shot up from the teens to more than 20, including a career high of 28.9 in 1970–71.

Havlicek's nickname may have been "Hondo" (inspired by the 1953 movie of the same name starring John Wayne), but it very easily could have been "Mr. Clutch." He was at his best when the game was on the line. Two years before his sensational shot that gave the Celtics a one-point lead late in the second overtime of Game 5 of the 1976 finals against Phoenix, he connected on another memorable shot. It came in the late stages of the first overtime of Game 6 of the finals with the Celtics trailing by two points at home against Kareem-Abdul Jabbar and the Milwaukee Bucks. "As far as wanting the ball, I felt that I could do something, which was going to give us a decent shot at winning the game or tying it," said Havlicek in the NBA TV video. "Don Chaney was able to deflect the ball, and I saw that there was only one person between myself and the basket, and that was Kareem. I knew that I could stop and pull up and take a shot from the free throw line. Unfortunately, I missed it. And as Kareem turned, it was such a bad shot, it shot right back over his head, and I followed through and put the ball in to tie it up and send it into the second overtime." In the second overtime, Havlicek scored nine of Boston's 11 points, including a shot that put his team up by one point with time running out. The Celtics eventually lost the game but recovered to win Game 7 in Milwaukee.

It was a defensive play, however, that just might go down as Havlicek's signature moment. It was Game 7 of the 1965 Eastern Division finals at home against the Philadelphia 76ers. Boston had a 110–109 lead with just five seconds remaining. Bill Russell was trying to inbound the ball underneath the Philadelphia basket with a chance for the Celtics to ice the game. But Russell stepped back, thought he could inbound the ball, but happened to be underneath a wire that attached to the balcony and the basket. And the rule was that, if the ball hit that wire, possession would go to the other team.

And that's s exactly what happened. Philadelphia got possession of the ball.

"As the play was unfolding and the official handed the ball to Hal Greer," said Havlicek in the NBA TV video, "I knew he had five seconds to get it in play, and I started counting to myself, 'One thousand one, one thousand two, one thousand three.' Nothing was happening, I took a little peek, and I realized he only had another second to put it in play." Havlicek knocked the inbounds pass to Sam Jones, who dribbled the ball until time ran out. "From that point on," Havlicek said in the video, "it was really a wild scene on the Boston Garden floor." His amazing defensive play prompted longtime Celtics radio announcer Johnny Most's legendary call, 'Havlicek stole the ball!'"

Born on April 8, 1940, in Martins Ferry, Ohio, Havlicek played basketball for Bridgeport High School in nearby Bridgeport, Ohio. He was a forward on Ohio State University teams that appeared in three consecutive NCAA title games his sophomore through senior years, including winning the 1960 contest. Havlicek's best season was his senior year in 1961–62 when he averaged 17 points and 9.7 rebounds per game.

Not only was Havlicek selected by Boston in the first round of the 1962 NBA Draft, he was also drafted by the NFL's Cleveland Browns that year. After competing briefly as a wide receiver in training camp that summer, he decided to focus on basketball. He played for the Celtics at small forward and shooting guard all the way through the 1977–78 season, including eight NBA championships. He led the NBA in minutes played per game in both 1970–71 and 1971–72. He was an All-Star 13 times and is a member of the Naismith Memorial Basketball Hall of Fame and the College Basketball Hall of Fame. He passed away on April 25, 2019, leaving behind his wife, Beth, a grown son, and a grown daughter.

Steve Kuberski

It was January 29, 1967. Steve Kuberski was a sophomore forward for the University of Illinois basketball team. That afternoon, the Illini were scheduled to take on number-one ranked UCLA in Chicago Stadium. "UCLA had Lew Alcindor (now Kareem Abdul-Jabbar)," said Kuberski, "but, because the NCAA claimed Illinois had a slush fund, which was funneling money indirectly to our players, our starting five players were suspended, and our head coach was fired."

Kuberski transferred to Bradley University and had to sit out his first year there. As a senior forward for the Braves, he led the team with averages of 23 points and 10.1 rebounds per game.

Born in Moline, Illinois, on November 6, 1947, Kuberski became interested in athletics when he was eight or nine years old. "We used to go to the park and play baseball pickup games," he said. "In the winter, we'd shovel off the courts and play outside basketball. Whatever sport that was in season, we'd play basically. I started playing Little League Baseball in fourth or fifth grade. Our grade school actually had a basketball team that played other grade schools in the surrounding towns. I played forward. I was a better baseball player than a basketball player. In baseball, I was a first baseman and pitcher. We had what we called a Babe Ruth League, which was above Little League as you got older. I was an all-star on that team. I played defensive end in football for two years in junior high, where in ninth grade I also played basketball."

Kuberski's favorite sport was baseball until he got to Moline High School in the tenth grade. "Between ninth and tenth grades," he said, "I had a growth spurt where I grew from about 5-11 or 6-foot to about 6-4 or 6-5. Then, all of a sudden, I started practicing basketball because I wanted to make the team. I said, 'Shoot, I'm not gonna make it unless I really practice hard.' So I did, and I ended up really playing well on the sophomore team. I averaged 15, 16 points per game as a forward and center. I continued growing and was one of the tallest kids on the team."

As a junior, Kuberski made the varsity team and averaged around 15 points per game at forward. As a senior, he played forward and center. He was 6-foot-6 1/2 by then. "I averaged 28, 29 points per game," he said. "We got to the quarterfinals of the state tournament and ended up losing to a team that we shouldn't have lost to. We were always ranked in the top three or four in the state. It was all one division back then. You were playing against some Chicago schools that had 4,000 boys in their schools. We weren't small. We had about 3,000 kids in my school."

Kuberski was recruited by 300 to 400 colleges. "It came down to Notre Dame and Illinois," he said. "Illinois was on TV where I was from. They had nice facilities. Assembly Hall was one of the first big, big new arenas for basketball—20,000 or so seats. I was captain of the freshman team at forward."

The 6-foot-8, 215-pound Kuberski was selected by Boston in the fourth round of the 1969 NBA Draft. "It was because of Celtics forward Don Nelson, who was from my hometown," he said. "We used to play ball together at the local YMCA in Moline. He told Red Auerbach, 'Red, you might as well take a flyer on this kid.'"

Kuberski, who returned to Bradley after his rookie season to earn his degree in business, was roommates with Celtics great John Havlicek in his second season of 1970–71. "John was a great mentor," he said. "He was unbelievable. His work ethic was incredible."

Chosen by New Orleans in the 1974 expansion draft, Kuberski wound up getting traded to Milwaukee. He was claimed off waivers by Buffalo before the 1975–76 season. Less than a month into the schedule, he was waived. Three weeks later, he signed as a free agent with Boston and returned to the Celtics, where he played until a couple months into the 1977–78 season when he was waived. He decided to retire. In 1981, he started his own company in Boston selling industrial warehouse equipment. After four or five years, the company began selling lockers to football stadiums, golf clubs, and high schools, then branched out from there. In 2014, Kuberski sold the business to one of his two grown sons. Kuberski lives with his wife, Diane, in Sanibel Island, Florida. He enjoys playing tennis, working out at the gym, and watching sports on television.

Kevin Stacom

Kevin Stacom was a gym rat while growing up in Queens, New York. "I was 5-foot-2 and 96 pounds when I started high school at Holy Cross in Flushing," he said. "But I loved to play basketball. I think the freshman coach kept me on the team as a sympathy move. I was the last guy on the bench. I was also the last guy on the junior varsity team's bench my sophomore year. There were millions of guys my age competing for places on the varsity team my junior year, so the competition was pretty fierce. We won the Catholic City League championship, but I still didn't get any meaningful playing time."

As a senior, Stacom finally got a chance to play. He started at shooting guard. "An injury gave me some playing time during the preseason," he said. "I got thrown into a game, and I was pretty eager to prove myself. I had a real good game and took off from there. I was a late developer. The benefit of that is that you have no choice but to be a guard, and as your body kicks in you can take those skills with you as a bigger guy."

Born in Manhattan, New York, on September 4, 1951, Stacom moved to Queens and then close to Belmont Park racetrack. His earliest memories are playing stickball with his older brother and friends. "I played Little League Baseball, CYO baseball, and CYO basketball," he said.

Stacom received a full scholarship to play basketball at Holy Cross University. "Jack Donohue, the Holy Cross head coach, knew that I was a gym rat, and that's why he recruited me," he said. "The assistant coach, Frank McCardle, was the guy who really vouched for me. I started at guard on the freshman team. We did okay. We were up and down. My sophomore year, again at guard, I was on the varsity team. I started maybe one or two games. I had a breakout game against Fordham, who was coached by future Notre Dame head coach Digger Phelps, that season. I couldn't be too cocky, though, because I wasn't a big high school star. I was indebted to the Holy Cross coaches because they gave me a chance."

After Stacom's sophomore year, he had a tough decision to make. "There was always a culture war on campus about the role of sports in regard to the school," he said. "There was a large segment—much of the faculty and administration— that wanted to de-emphasize sports. But that's not what I was working for, so I got a little nervous."

Stacom transferred to Providence College. He had to sit out a year before he played. He started at guard in 1972–73 and 1973–74. "The guard who'd played my position had graduated, so I stepped right in," he said. "Also, the year I became eligible to play, they opened up the Civic

Center in Providence, the largest venue in New England at the time. It seated 11,000, 12,000 people. We had two first-team All-Americans—Marvin Barnes and Ernie DiGregorio—in '72–'73."

The Friars not only played in the NCAA tournament that season, they advanced all the way to the Final Four, losing to Memphis State (now Memphis) in the semifinals. "We were up by 16 points when Marvin hyperextended his knee," Stacom said. "We didn't give up, though, but we knew our goose was kind of cooked. We would've definitely been in the finals had Marvin not gotten hurt and would've played UCLA in the finals." Stacom, who scored 15 points in that game, averaged 17.8 points per contest that year in helping Providence to a 27–4 record. The next season, he averaged 18.5 points and a team-leading 5.3 assists per game in helping his team to a 28–4 mark and qualification for the NCAA tourney again. This time, the Friars fell to top-ranked, and eventual champion, North Carolina State with Tom Burleson and David Thompson in an East Regional semifinal. "We were tied with four minutes to go, but then they fouled me and Marvin out of the game. It was the only game I ever fouled out in my entire life," Stacom said. "That season, it was just Marvin, myself, and a number of younger players. Marvin was a great, great talent and a great teammate."

As for his chances of a career in the NBA, it was always in the back of Stacom's mind. "I always thought I had a shot at the NBA," he said, "even when I was the last guy on the bench my freshman year in high school. I was a bit of a dreamer, so that was my goal."

The 6-foot-3, 185-pound Stacom, who had been drafted by Chicago in the second round of the 1973 NBA Draft but instead chose to return to school for his senior season (he majored in English), was drafted by Boston in the second round in 1974. He was also drafted by the ABA's New York Nets that year. "It was an easy decision for me to choose Boston over New York," he said. "For my type of game, I didn't think I'd fit in in the ABA. They were trying to market themselves with the three-point shot and a lot of one-on-one type of stuff. They had talent in that league, but I thought I'd fit in better with more of a team-oriented league. I was always a Celtic fan, even growing up in New York. I was pretty lucky to be going to play for Boston."

According to Stacom, who was a reserve for most of his NBA career, in his rookie season it was all about having a one-track mind. "You had to focus when you got into a game," he said. "You couldn't be too impressed by anything because you had to compete against those other great players and great athletes. It was an older team. A lot of guys were married with kids, so it was a little maddening for sure. It was an established team, so you had to earn the players' respect, and the only way to do that was to do your job. I thought I worked as hard as I could. I caught the end of a great era, including winning the championship in 1976. John Havlicek, Don Nelson, Paul Silas, Don Chaney, Jo Jo White, Dave Cowens … they were great people, just an unbelievable group of guys. They weren't big talkers, they all lived by example, and they were just a bunch of very unique, quality people. It was great to be around them. Red Auerbach was an unusual guy. I got a kick out of him. He was good company. He was always open to BSing. I thought he was a good man."

During the summer of 1978, Stacom signed as a free agent with Indiana but then was sold back to the Celtics on February 9, 1979. He retired for a couple of seasons and got into the bar-restaurant business in Newport, Rhode Island, as a partner. By 1981, Nelson, his ex-teammate with the Celtics, was the Milwaukee Bucks' head coach. "He had a bunch of injuries and asked me to come and play for him," said Stacom, who played very briefly with the Bucks in 1981–82 before retiring for good. Stacom wound up being a partner in four restaurants in Newport. He got out of the business in 2017. He had also began scouting for NBA teams in the early 1980s with Milwaukee. He also scouted for Golden State and presently is a scout for Dallas. "There's a lot of traveling with scouting, but the positives outweigh the negatives," he said.

Stacom lives in Saunderstown, Rhode Island, with his wife, Karen. He has two grown children from a previous marriage. His hobbies are reading and working out. "The type of player I was, I had to work pretty hard at it," he said, "so I always enjoyed working out, and I've kept that up."

Glenn McDonald

When Glenn McDonald was drafted by the Boston Celtics in 1974, he was not exactly thrilled. "One of my assistant coaches at Long Beach State called me and told me that I'd been drafted by the Celtics in the first round," he said. "I told him, 'Okay, thanks for calling me, but I'm in the middle of moving right now.' And he just went berserk. He said, 'Did you hear what I just told you? I told you that you just got drafted by the Boston Celtics!' I said, 'I know, coach, but I'm moving. I'm trying to move my stuff into another apartment. I'll call you back later.' It felt good, but at the same time, I knew I was going to have to leave California and go to Boston. The other thing was, I always hated Boston because they won all the time. I'm a person who roots for underdogs. So I wasn't really that pleased to go to Boston. It didn't really sink in to what had happened until I went to Boston for a visit and to see the Garden, talk to Red Auerbach, and look up and see all the banners. It suddenly hit me that this is something very, very special, and maybe I can end up getting a ring one day."

McDonald's long road to the Celtics began when he was born on March 18, 1952, in Kewanee, Illinois. He gained an interest in athletics when he was around 11 years old. "I ran track and played football and was always one of the better athletes," he said. "I was really fast, I could jump, and I had great endurance."

McDonald's mother dropped a bomb on her son when he was 13 years old. "She decided to move to California during the Watts riots, and I didn't want to go to California during that time," he said. "She wanted me to come. She also wanted me to be involved with sports, but I told her that, when we get to California, I wasn't playing any sports as a punishment to her for moving me out there. I played on the playgrounds, and was pretty good, but not in organized team sports. On one of the playgrounds, a kid two years older than me challenged me—he was an All-American at Jefferson High School in Los Angeles—and asked me if I was going to come try out for the basketball team because the next year I was going to be in high school as a sophomore. I told him that I wasn't going to play. He told me I probably wouldn't even make the 'C' team, which was the lowest, anyway. So I said to myself, 'Wait a minute. He's telling me that I can't make that 'C' team?' So I went out for the team and made it and became a starter on the varsity team. I started at small forward and shooting guard all three years. I was the leading scorer and one of the top rebounders on the team my senior year. My last year, I averaged right around 28 points and 11 rebounds per game. We always made it to the semifinals or finals but never won the city championship."

Besides Long Beach State, other colleges that recruited McDonald—his sophomore year! —included USC, North Carolina, North Carolina State, and Maryland. "I chose Long Beach State because I wanted to stay near home. That was the biggest reason," he said. "The other reason was that I wanted to go to a school that I thought had a chance to beat UCLA because Jerry Tarkanian, the head coach there, was bringing in some good players at that time. I just liked how he was as a person. It was fun playing under him. I liked his assistant coaches as well. He just had a blend of people around us who seemed like they cared about us not just as basketball players but as people in general."

After playing on the freshman team as the leading scorer in 1970–71, McDonald became a starter at small forward on the varsity team midway through his sophomore season. "We were playing against the University of Pacific, and one of their guards lit us up for about 32, 33 points," he recalled. "We played them again less than three weeks later, and some of our players were telling Tark that 'if you let Glenn play, *he* could guard that kid.' So Tark put me in the starting lineup that game, and I held that guy to six points. And, from that point on, I was the starter and became a defensive player. From being an offensive player in high school, I became a defensive stopper throughout my college career. In high school, we were known for our defense even though we had good scorers. When I went into the defensive role in college, it wasn't really a big deal for me. I knew we had people who could put the ball in the basket. So whenever we played against a really good offensive player, that's who I had to guard." McDonald helped the 49ers (now the Beach) to a 25–4 record but a loss to top-ranked UCLA in the West Regional final of the NCAA tournament. Even though we lost, it was a good experience playing against a team like UCLA. Overall, it was a great game. We knew so many of the different players on the team because they'd come down to Long Beach in the summer—[Bill] Walton and all of those guys—and play."

The next season, McDonald helped Long Beach State to a 26–3 record and another appearance in the NCAA tourney that ended with a defeat to the University of San Francisco in the West Regional semifinals. In his senior season under new head coach Lute Olson, he averaged 13.4 points and 4.5 rebounds per game. The 49ers finished 24–2 but were put on probation a couple games into the season, thus barring them from postseason play. "I enjoyed playing under Lute," said McDonald. "He tried to be a little sterner than Tark. Tark was a little bit looser. But Lute kind of opened up the offense a little more where we could be a little bit more athletic, whereas Tark was stuck on the zone defense. He didn't really like to let us get out and run on the fast break. It was more controlled."

Halfway through McDonald's senior season, he learned the Celtics and Bucks were looking at him. "From what I heard," he said, "they just thought I was tall, I was long, I played defense, and I could shoot the ball. I think they liked that I was somebody they could rely on while I was on the floor. My rookie season, pretty much all of the Celtics—Don Nelson, John Havlicek, Jo Jo White—just kind of mentored me and showed me what it was all about as far as professionalism."

The 6-foot-6, 190-pound McDonald spent two seasons with Boston as a backup—including an NBA title in 1975–76—before getting waived at the start of the 1976–77 season. He signed with Milwaukee on November 12, 1976, but was waived three and a half weeks later. He played in Sweden in 1977–78 and in the Philippines from '78 through 1984. He then retired. He returned to Long Beach State and, for the next 11 years, was an assistant coach for the men's team and an assistant coach and head coach for the women's team. Then he became the intramural director through 2018 when he retired for good. McDonald and his wife, Renee, live in Long Beach. They have a grown son, grown daughter, and two grandchildren. "I help out with the nearby Lakewood Special Olympics," he said. "I'm not a golfer, but I enjoy going to the driving range and hitting balls. I like going to the movies, too."

McDonald believes that God has a plan for everybody. "Maybe his plan for me was, 'I'll let you get a taste of this, but I'm not gonna let you stay there long. Let's see what you do when I say it's time for your playing career to be over,'" he said. "I know guys who didn't get a chance to play in the NBA, and they just went to the wayside. God asked, 'Are you going to be that kind of person? Are you going to find something else to do?' It was a good career even though it was only three years. I feel blessed to have played for three years. If I'd just gone to training camp, I'd have been blessed. But to play a few seasons and win a championship … what more can you really ask for?"

Don Nelson

It's hard to decide whether Don Nelson had a better playing career or coaching career in the NBA. He was an excellent player for three teams, mainly the Boston Celtics, for 14 seasons. He was a tremendous head coach for four teams over the course of 31 seasons. He is the NBA's all-time leader in wins for head coaches with 1,335. He is a member of the Naismith Memorial Basketball Hall of Fame as a coach. So, although he had a magnificent career as a player, it is probably safe to say that he had an even better career as a head coach.

Nelson's path to basketball stardom began when he was born on May 15, 1940, in Muskegon, Michigan. He grew up on a farm in Illinois. "I went to a one-room schoolhouse," he said in his Hall of Fame speech. "There were nine grades, there were six students. I was the only kid in my class. Two of the other students were my sisters. My uncle Walt bought a basket and a basketball for me and put it up in the chicken yard and didn't know really how tall it was supposed to be, so he put it up 11 feet. He thought that looked about right, so I started shooting on a basket 11 feet tall. I learned how to play a little bit out there. My neighbor a couple of miles down the way came over and played one-on-one with me once in a while."

After Nelson's family lost its farm, the clan moved to Rock Island, Illinois, where Don started playing organized basketball. "I started out in the YMCA," he said in his Hall of Fame speech. "When I first started, I was the guy that never got picked. Spending all day there, I learned how to play a little bit, and before the summer was over, I was the first guy picked on the team."

Nelson played basketball for Rock Island High School. He led the Rocks to 25–3 and 22–4 records, respectively, in his junior and senior years. He scored 39 points and had 20 rebounds against Moline (Illinois) High and had 30 points and 29 rebounds against top-ranked Ottawa (Illinois) High. He was not heavily recruited, and wound up at the University of Iowa, whose head coach, Sharm Scheuerman, was a graduate of Rock Island. Nelson led the Hawkeyes in points per game and rebounds per game his sophomore through senior years. His best season was his last, 1961–62, when he netted 23.8 points and 11.9 rebounds per contest. All three seasons, Iowa had winning records, the best of which was 18–6 his junior year.

The 6-foot-6, 210-pound Nelson was a third-round pick by the Chicago Zephyrs (now Washington Wizards) in the 1962 NBA Draft. He spent his rookie season playing forward, where he would remain for the rest of his career. "My first coach was Jack McMahon," he said on a Warriors TV show. "I loved him dearly. He was a big influence in my life, a guy that taught me how to love the game and how to be a factor as a smart player."

Nelson was claimed on waivers by the Los Angeles Lakers on September 6, 1963. He spent two playoff seasons with the Lakers, including a loss to the Celtics in the NBA Finals his second season with them. "I got a chance to play with Jerry West and Elgin Baylor," he said on the Warriors TV show.

After the Lakers did not re-sign him for the 1965–66 season, Nelson was sitting at home not knowing what he was going to do. "I got a phone call from Red Auerbach," he said in his Hall of Fame speech. "He said, 'We're looking for a forward, [Tom] Heinsohn just retired, would you like a tryout?' I'm on the next plane, I can't wait to get to Boston. And the guys that took me under their wings—Bill Russell, K. C. Jones, Sam Jones—those guys made me feel welcome right away."

Nelson spent 11 seasons—through 1975–76—with Boston, mainly as the sixth man off the bench. He was rock solid, averaging 11.4 points and 5.2 rebounds per game. His best season was 1969–70 when he netted 15.4 points and 7.3 rebounds per contest. He was an integral part of five Celtics championship teams, the first three of which came against his old team, the Lakers. Nelson connected on a crucial jump shot down the stretch in Game 7 of the 1969 finals against Los Angeles. "I spent an awful lot of time with Red [Auerbach] over the years trying to understand the game and how to not coach it at that point but how to play it better," he said in an interview on Warriors TV. "I had a good teacher in Red."

Nelson's jersey number, 19, is retired by the Celtics. Said Nelson on a CBS Sports telecast in 1983, "I think that it probably meant more to me than most of the players who are up there because to have an average player's number retired … I've never heard of such a thing. I'm very proud of that."

After retiring, Nelson needed a job. He was raising four children. "I was looking around for something to do, and I thought maybe a natural would be to be a referee," he said on the Warriors TV show. "So I went out to the [NBA Los Angeles] Summer League, and I tried that for a while. I really liked that actually. I thought I would be a good referee."

But then, out of the blue, came an opportunity to join the Milwaukee Bucks as an assistant coach under Larry Costello in 1976–77. "I grabbed it," he said on the Warriors TV show.

"I was kind of just the luckiest guy in America, just in the right place at the right time," Nelson said. "They needed a young guy along with an older kind of a coach and thought that I'd be the perfect fit. Larry resigned after 18 games. We had lost 15 of 18. I turned the job down three times because I certainly wasn't ready to be a head coach. I actually wanted to be an assistant for Jack Ramsay [with Portland] before I tried to become a head coach to gain the experience. But it was something the [Bucks'] owner at that time, Jim Fitzgerald, wanted me to do and just said, 'Look, we understand you don't know what you're doing yet, but we're willing to work with you and we want you to be our guy, and just do the best you can,' so that's how I got started. My first team, I just said, 'Hey look, I'm not going to lie to anybody here. I'm your new head coach, I don't have a clue what I'm doing, but we're going to do it the way the Celtics did it.' And that's how we started. I ran a lot of their plays, I had the defensive setups and concepts that they had, and they were all solid concepts, and we just went from there."

Under Nelson's guidance, Milwaukee improved from a 30–52 record in 1976–77 to a 44–38 mark and a playoff berth in 1977–78. During the next nine seasons, the Bucks were playoff regulars with players such as Marques Johnson, Sidney Moncrief, and big Bob Lanier. "We were the best defensive team in the league then," Nelson said in the Warriors TV interview. Three times, the Bucks advanced all the way to the Eastern Conference finals, and three times they lost. "My teams in Milwaukee were the best teams that I coached through my career," Nelson said. "Unfortunately, there were two other better teams in the East. One was the Philadelphia 76ers with Moses Malone and Dr. J. and, of course, everybody knows the Larry Bird teams with McHale and those teams. We actually beat both of those teams in the playoffs but not in the same year, so we never made the finals."

Nelson's last year as Milwaukee's head coach was in 1986–87. Two years later, he became Golden State's head coach. He improved the Warriors from 20–62 the season before to a 43–39 record and advancement to the second round of the playoffs. Three more times, including a 55-win season in 1991–92, he led Golden State to postseason berths through his last season in 1994–95. He won 34 of 59 games as the head coach of the Knicks in 1995–96, and then after a year off, became the head coach of the Dallas Mavericks. He improved the Mavs from the depths of despair to a perennial playoff contender, including a 60–22 record and an appearance in the Western Conference finals in 2002–03. His last season with Dallas was in 2004–05. Perhaps Nelson's most memorable experience was when he returned to Golden State in 2006–07 and led the team to a 42–40 mark and their first playoff appearance in 13 years. That season, they were the eighth and final seed in the Western Conference playoffs but shocked the top-seeded Mavericks (67–15) in the first round of the playoffs. "That was a very exciting time for us," he said in the Warriors TV interview. He coached Golden State through the 2009–10 season before retiring.

"Every team that I coached stands out because, if you're going to write my M.O., it's going to be that I've taken bad teams and made good ones out of them [except New York]," said Nelson. "Each team in its development became a good team and became a special team for me."

Nelson may have never won an NBA title as a coach, but he did lead Team USA, known as "Dream Team II", to the gold medal at the 1994 FIBA World Championship in Toronto.

"A good coach," said Nelson in the Warriors TV interview, "will take whatever team he has, evaluate it, and play to its potential, and try to get the best out of his team where you can win the most games and go the farthest in the playoffs and maybe have a chance to win a title."

Early in his coaching career, Nelson had several assistants who went on to do quite well in NBA head coaching jobs. "And they used a lot of my philosophies in understanding the game the way I thought it should be played," he continued. "And they carried that along with their philosophy and their teams. [San Antonio head coach] Gregg Popovich is the best example because he's been coaching the best teams, but there are many other players and assistant coaches that I've had and ended up going on to coach in the league. And the most important part as far as I'm concerned is that those guys are making a good living in the league, and I had a little something to do with it."

How does Nelson want to be remembered?

"Not as a Hall of Famer for sure, just a hard-working schmo that basically tried to get the best out of his team and tried to do a good job," he said in the Warriors TV interview. "If you reflect on my career and say, 'That guy was a good coach,' that's enough for me."

Jim Ard

Jim Ard was getting nowhere in his high school basketball career. He was stuck on the bench as a reserve. "The first high school I went to was in Joliet, Illinois. Here I was a freshman and then a sophomore, and I got my butt kicked because those guys played rough. I had to learn how to play," he said. "I was put on the varsity team because I was one of the taller kids, about 6-foot-5. We moved to Markham, Illinois, and I went to Thornton High School in nearby Harvey. I joined the varsity team my junior year and was mostly a center or forward." Ard did not get to play much, so he made a concerted effort to play against junior college kids and pros in pickup games on different public courts the following summer to improve his skills. "That helped my game tremendously," he said. "I figured out what I had to do to be a starter. My senior year I started at center. We won the Illinois state championship for the bigger schools. I was probably the second-leading scorer on my team."

Born in Seattle on September 19, 1948, Ard attended junior high school in the town of Richland, Washington. He played Little League Baseball but, when his father put a basketball hoop and backboard up in the driveway, basketball soon became his sport of choice. "That's how I got started in basketball," he said. "That's the sport I began to get close to."

Colleges that recruited Ard included Indiana, Kansas, and Cincinnati. He chose Cincinnati. "I played on the freshman team as the starting center. We did very well," he said. "The only team that I can remember that we lost to was Kentucky, and they had seven high school All-Americans. My sophomore and junior years I played forward, and I played center my senior year. We had pretty good teams." Ard averaged both a team-leading 19.2 points and 15.2 rebounds per game his senior year in leading the Bearcats to a 21–6 record. He majored in marketing.

The 6-foot-8, 215-pound Ard was selected by his hometown team of Seattle in the first round of the 1970 NBA Draft. He was also drafted by the ABA's New York Nets. "With Seattle," he said, "it looked like signing me was going to be a long, drawn out process, and my feeling was that I needed to keep playing basketball without having to worry about a contract. So I decided to see what the ABA had to offer, and I took it. That was the best decision for me." Ard was mainly a backup center throughout his entire professional career. After spending three seasons with the Nets, he was traded to the ABA's Memphis Tams and played for them in 1973–74. He signed as a free agent with the Boston Celtics a couple of weeks before the start of the 1974–75 season. "Thank goodness for the Celtics," he said. "They were absolutely great to me. The guys accepted me immediately." He spent a little more than three seasons with Boston, including winning the 1975–76 NBA title. He concluded his career with the Bulls in 1977–78. He was released prior to the start of the following season and then retired.

Ard worked for several high-tech companies and networking companies before retiring for good in 2011. He and his wife, Maureen, live in Discovery Bay, California. He has two grown children from a previous marriage. He enjoys salmon fishing, water aerobics, and his 40-foot motorhome.

RECOLLECTIONS OF GAME 5 OF THE 1976 NBA FINALS

Jerry Colangelo
"If that game was not the greatest game of all time, it's certainly one of the two or three greatest games of all time."

Alvan Adams (from the June 3, 2001, *Boston Globe*)
"People remember this game fondly in Phoenix, but I always say, 'We lost the game. We lost the series.' But there's no denying it was an incredible game. There were great plays, right to the end."

Tom Heinsohn
"It was the greatest game I ever was involved in with the Celtics."

Dave Cowens (from the June 3, 2001, *Boston Globe*)
"It's wonderful to say you were involved in a game that was one of the greatest in the history of our sport, and that you were a pivotal player. It's an honor in itself. Of course, you don't know it while you're doing it."

John MacLeod (from *Great Moments in the NBA: Awesome Endings*)
"That was the greatest game I've ever been involved in."

Dick Van Arsdale
"It was the greatest game I was ever a part of."

Jo Jo White (from the LATV show *Cityscope*)
I don't know about the greatest, I know it was one of the longest.

Nate Hawthorne (from the June 3, 2001, *Boston Globe*)

"I only played three seasons and this was the highlight of my career. It's kind of hard to forget."

Bob Ryan

"It was a game that had so much packed into it with the momentum swings in regulation and then all the drama of the overtimes. The other thing was that Phoenix wasn't supposed to be there. So you could look at it and say, 'Well, it wasn't that big a deal because it wasn't against the best team, it wasn't against Golden State.' And some people have criticized the game and have said, 'You can't say it's one of the greatest games ever because it didn't match up two titans. It wasn't the Celtics and the Warriors.' Well, that's one way of looking at it. To me, the fact that the upstart Suns were doing this and keeping pace with and putting the pressure on the Celtics, and this was an expansion team eight years into its existence, was remarkable. The nature of some of the stuff that happened in the game like the drama of Heard's shot, Westphal's amazing, spinning, 360-degree shot, and then finally Glenn McDonald being the ultimate hero was just tremendous. There were so many great things in the game. Was it the greatest game ever? It might be. It's held up very well with other games. I know one thing—it was 10 years minimum before there was any finals game that even approached it."

Dennis Awtrey (from the June 3, 2001, *Boston Globe*)

"I'm not sure it was the best played game, but if you're talking about twists and turns, yeah, it was the best game I was ever in. I never played in a game as important or as hard fought."

Steve Kuberski

"I thought some of the games we played against the great Knicks teams in the early '70s were probably better played games than this one, but it was probably the most exciting game I was ever a part of."

Ricky Sobers (from the June 3, 2001, *Boston Globe*)

"I can say I played in the greatest game in the history of basketball."

Glenn McDonald

"It was, for sure, the greatest game I was ever involved in or have seen, especially because it was in the championship series. For me to have been involved in a game like this … it was just unbelievable. I never came close to being involved in anything close to that. It's definitely tops on my list."

Paul Westphal

"It's hard to say it isn't the greatest game I was ever a part of as a player or coach. I was in a triple-overtime game against the Bulls *coaching* in the finals, but that game probably didn't have quite as many ups and downs as this game. The other thing about this game is that it was before TiVo, it was before … you didn't get all the games. It was a big deal to watch an NBA playoff game, so the meaning that was attached to the game coast-to-coast and through the way television was, it probably is hard to top."

Don Nelson (from the June 3, 2001, *Boston Globe*)

"I would have to rate that game as the No. 1 of all I played. I remember all the big shots."

Charlie Scott

"It was a phenomenal game."

Phil Lumpkin (from the June 3, 2001, *Boston Globe*)

"From time to time, I catch it on TV and reminisce. But it's more important to my parents. I throw it in my kids' faces. I say, 'I realized my dream. I can help you with yours.'"

Gar Heard

"That game has to rank as the most memorable of all the games I was ever a part of, no question about it. It's something people still talk about all these years later."

John Havlicek (from *Great Moments in the NBA: Awesome Endings*)

"There were so many highs and lows. You thought you had it won, and all of a sudden you were elated. Within a second, it would turn around, and you thought you were defeated."

Paul Silas (from the June 3, 2001, *Boston Globe*)

"Undoubtedly, that was the most significant game I was ever involved in, and I've been involved in a bunch of 'em."

Kevin Stacom

"I think it was the greatest game I was ever a part of. It was a triple-overtime finals game, and it was in the happy, old Garden. It was very unusual, very intense, just a great game all-around."

Walt Frazier (from Classic Sports Network)

"Doing it at the fabled Boston Garden, which is why I think this game is voted one of the greatest ever, you have a sort of David and Goliath here and the Suns rising to the occasion not once, not twice, but three times and almost pulling it off."

Al McCoy

"There have been two triple-overtime games in the NBA Finals. The Suns have been involved in both—the one in '76 and the one in '93 in Chicago that the Suns won against Michael Jordan and the Bulls. But from a sheer emotional standpoint, the '76 game was the most memorable. In '93, the Suns were expected to win. They had the best record in the NBA, they had Charles Barkley, Kevin Johnson, and Dan Majerle. They were more or less expected to be there. In '76, the team was not expected to be there, and that triple-overtime game would be what I would call the greatest game that I've ever broadcast. It was a classic."

Red Auerbach (from the June 3, 2001, *Boston Globe*)

"The best game I ever saw."

Rick Barry

"It was one of the most exciting games ever, an incredibly exciting game."

Curtis Perry (from the June 3, 2001, *Boston Globe*)

"People say to me, 'What's the best game you ever saw?' And I say, 'Well, there was this night in June, back in Boston…'"

Printed in the United States
By Bookmasters